WORK LIFE

WORKING REMOTELY
FROM BALI TO BOARDROOM

Published in Canada, for Global Distribution by YGTMedia Co.
www.ygtmedia.co/publishing

To order additional copies of this book: publishing@ygtmedia.co

Edited by Kelly Lamb

Interior design and typesetting by Doris Chung

Cover design by Michelle Fairbanks

eBook by Ellie Sipilä

Author Photo by Qian Hao

TORONTO

WORK LIFE

WORKING REMOTELY
FROM BALI TO BOARDROOM

MELINDA JACOBS

For my family

TABLE OF CONTENTS

INTRODUCTION

Four years ago, I found myself in the heart of digital nomad subculture, running a coworking space in Bali. I started writing about my experiences as a way of unpacking what I was seeing and making sense of what pieces of this emergent subculture I wanted to build into whatever my next steps would be. Did I want a job, or did I want to keep working from the jungle or beach? Could I have the career I wanted in those circumstances? Would that mean a job or contract work? In what ways would that be limiting? The sex appeal of the digital nomads was that their work lives were tightly bound with the pursuit of pleasure—a nice meal, leisure time, sports, activities, and experiences—that weighed life with the same importance as work. Work could be fulfilling, sure, but it was not enough. Freedom to define happiness outside of work was the ultimate prize—and one that could be pursued voraciously and head on. Remote work, or telecommuting, has been a style of working since the 1970s, but no group has spurned the norms of work life and fully embraced the potential of working online to the extent of the digital nomads.

There is no piece of remote work that doesn't seem to border other topics in the evolution, or the devolution, of the traditional workplace, nine-to-fives, daily commutes, and the structures of rigidity we used to associate with having a desk job. And along with these changes, we've expanded our vocabulary to include Zoom, hybrid meetings, and an increasingly casual workforce (or "gig work"). The subculture of digital nomads, long-term remote workers who work and travel simultaneously, has reached the mainstream, catalyzed by a pandemic that forced a rethinking and reengineering of what it means to go to work. In a pandemic-era world, the norms of remote work are applying to more and more workplaces, changing what it means to "go" to work for about 50 percent of knowledge workers. The "how" questions are getting answered by management professionals and influencers who tell you how to do it better (whatever that may mean). But after two or more years of forced remote work—working from home or living at work—many are still asking if remote work is something they like. Without the choice, remote work can feel disconnected and lonely.

When I first started writing this book, it was meant as an antidote to the "how to" manuals and evangelical texts that praised remote work as the savior to the individual who felt unhappy in the confines of their bricks and mortar workplace. What I didn't know when I started writing this was that remote work was actually about the pursuit of freedom, and the many different ways people harness remote work as a way of pursuing it. The digital nomads were simply the furthest along the journey.

Eventually, I took a job and went to an office for a few short months before the pandemic. Freedom within this "normal" work life was the ability (sort of) to leave work behind and to try to have a fully separated work and personal life in a way that allowed each to thrive. I don't think I mastered this part, and I don't know if I ever will—or have the opportunity to. Remote work, for me, was normal. It was those months in an office that felt borderline subversive to the psychology I had developed while pursuing my freedom outside of the walls of an office and outside of my relationship with an employer. I was more surprised by what I learned about myself during those months of in-office work, particularly my own reluctance to say and believe "this is it." I knew, consciously or not, that I'd gotten on a treadmill that was harder and harder to slow down.

But the tools and practices of remote work still applied in my traditional office space—the extent to which the availability of internet-based tools that had fostered collaboration within teams and firms had shrunk the distances between workers on either side of the country and made even the most traditional office more virtualized. My lifestyle during that time was very rooted. But my work, for better or worse, was still mostly online. And despite having a designated workspace, my attention was increasingly "at work"—which meant, on Slack, email, and Zoom calls.

I left my "normal" job mid-pandemic and started a life that was intentionally remote-first. This was like building a puzzle; a time with a lot of internal change while I sat in my apartment, free of the sorts of external stimuli that had guided previous transitions. This time, my work–life transition was an inside job.

Freedom now, as I look at the opportunities for remote work currently and into the future, is different. There are many decisions I've had to make now without an anchor, be that a job, an office, or a partner—deciding where to plant roots, without consideration of where my work is located. Some would not call this freedom; in fact, it involves a lot of decision-making. But it is one freedom that I have *only* because my career is not a constraining factor. I can truly work from anywhere.

The further into the journey I went, the more my questions shifted from the "why" and "why not" of remote work to the "how." That's evident in this book, too, as the pandemic normalized and mainstreamed remote work to an extent that was inconceivable when I started writing. Despite this, there are still many people and organizations debating the "why" (or "if" they should allow remote work in the long term). And there are new and evolving best practices on the "how." This book engages in those debates but isn't prescriptive—management practices for remote teams are different by function and industry, the extent to which asynchronous work is practical and applied, and many other factors. I have my guesses as to where these trends or practices will land, but like any reader, I mostly care about the parts that apply to me. The "why," though, will remain an open question until one can truly live a life in the knowledge economy without building a résumé of "traditional" work experience, or until one can move jobs virtually as openly as moving jobs in person. Much like confining a job search to a city with physical office spaces, many companies have yet to make a final call on the long-term viability of remote work, so searching for a 100 percent remote job does still seem to limit the available pool of employers (more or less so depending on profession).

The pandemic didn't seem to end but to fade into the background, and life found a new rhythm that I controlled the pace of—at work and outside of it. The particulars I engage with are of my life and the lives of people I met while working remotely. The context of the shifting world around us, of course, impacted my reporting and the scope at which the "trend" of remote work applied. The number of people working remotely has exploded.

The very concept of remote work has been so normalized since I started chronicling my own experiences and those of others that I worried if there was even a story anymore. Is the value and desirability of remote work such a self-evident truth that no one will be interested? Instead, what I've come to realize is that the gap between the reader and the people in the book has been made smaller. We're now all more fluent in the tools and tactics of remote work, and we've probably begun to make decisions that include the availability of remote work. As a result, I spend less time explaining the concepts of remote work, asynchronous work, and teleworking than I initially planned, and more time around the why I and many others choose—and sometime, struggle—to work remotely. I'm focused on the sorts of why questions that pulled me and many others around the world: Where do I belong? Could my life be better somewhere else?

I'm completing this writing from a different country than my employer, in a home that is fully optimized for remote work, and having fully shifted my personal focus from the "why" to the "how" of a fully remote career. I hope that in reading this book you'll have a better sense of how remote work can (or maybe cannot) apply to your work and a sense of opportunity in that discovery. There is so much life to live beyond the office, away from the screen.

CHAPTER 1

WELCOME BREAKFAST

The sound of cicadas was almost deafening. They woke me like an alarm, with a relentless, rolling chirp. Outside on the streets of Ubud, Bali, monkeys crisscrossed the power lines over the street. Making eye contact would entice them to reach for my phone or glasses in hopes of trading for food. A plastic bag made a ready target; I knew better than the tourists, who were easy prey.

I was one of the many digital nomads that flocked to the island to live and work in paradise. By October 2018, I'd already worked remotely for over five years. I'd never been required to work from an office Monday to Friday and used the flexibility to work from coffee shops and coworking spaces. In San Francisco, I'd blended in among the throng of office workers, my way of working indiscernible. In Bali, my floral shorts and tank top blended in with the tourists I walked past to approach a hand-carved sign that read "Hubud: Coworking and Café."

"Hubud" was a portmanteau of "hub" and "Ubud," the town made famous by Elizabeth Gilbert's bestselling *Eat Pray Love*. For many remote workers, Ubud (*ooo-buhd*) served as a similar turning point—there was *before* you visited Ubud, and *after*. Ubud was the place where transformation happened.

Above a drugstore, nestled at the top of a hidden staircase, Hubud didn't look like an office. You left your shoes at the door before entering, received a greeting from the welcome desk, and found a seat. There were big communal tables, modern desk chairs, and yoga balls. The main room had large stationary fans and the soft din of chitchat between coworkers and new friends, who floated among unassigned seats. If you wanted AC, there were two quiet, library-like spaces where you could cool down and do focused work. Since opening in 2012, Hubud had hosted over nine thousand members from more than eighty-five countries, a United Nations of remote workers in a bamboo building. There was a café on the outdoor patio that served coconut milk lattes and all-day brunch. Some people passed through Hubud for a day or two during a vacation; others came to work for months at a time. A few members had been in the space for years.

The jungle's humid climate had made me a morning person, and I often arrived before even the staff at the welcome desk. Each morning I sat facing a rice paddy and slowly settled into my email. The serenity was interrupted around ten o'clock, when the café ran the espresso machine, readying itself for members who trickled in from the street. The premium Hubud put on coffee was one of the few things it shared with urban coworking spaces, where small teams and startup companies worked in little hives of activity.

At Hubud, the members were digital nomads, often traveling alone with their work, for themselves or a company, in tow. "Be careful with your phone," the café staff warned, gesturing toward the monkeys who often wandered over in search of food or valuables to steal. It was hard to feel like I was "at work" when monkeys were part of the ambience.

Every Tuesday, there was a welcome breakfast for new members, an orientation of sorts to Hubud, the physical space, and the social networks within it. Tuesdays were my weekly chance to take the pulse of the space, to meet who was replacing who had left, and to learn who would fill the holes in my social life. It felt like life restarted every Tuesday morning, and that October morning was no different.

At about five minutes before ten, the café staff brought baskets of banana bread, dragon fruit, and papaya to the conference room, and I took that as my cue to pack up and move. I picked up a basket and lined it with a banana leaf, which would later be disposed of (to save washing the basket) and served myself. October was the shoulder season for tropical coworking; I didn't know that the membership would ebb and flow to the rhythm of North American and European winters. The occupancy was lower, and the community felt tighter in the lead-up to December, when the space would be filled to the brim with the remote-work equivalent of snowbirds.

Just after ten, the community manager declared it time to get started. "Welcome, everyone," he said, elongating the last syllable like *wonnn*. "Welcome to Hubud! I'm Kasyfi, like 'cash' and 'fee,'" he said rubbing his right fingers together. "Just think of money."

Kash was gregarious and effusive and had none of the awkwardness of the newcomers at the breakfast. His job was to encourage social connectivity and manufacture serendipity—to ensure that the right people met each other, that everyone had a friend. "I'm from Jakarta and lucky enough to live in beautiful Bali," Kash continued. "I've been working here for . . . two years? Yeah, and I'm so happy to meet you all, and we can be best friends." He was not being sarcastic; members really were among his best friends. Kash had never been out of Indonesia, and yet he had friends around the world—personal touch points who furnished him with Western pop and internet cultural literacy. In return, Kash and the other ten or so Indonesians who ran the space were an entry point into Indonesian, if not Balinese, culture for coworking members. Administratively similar but culturally and religiously distinct from the other six-thousand inhabited islands that make up the Indonesian archipelago, Bali is exotic, even within its own country.

"Just say your name, where you're from, and what brought you here," Kash encouraged. We were only a few people around the table, a number that increased to ten or even fifteen during high season.

"Hi, I'm Syed," the next person said. An affable man in his early forties, Syed was visiting from California as part of a manufacturing trip for his invention, an acupressure device. The trip was a test run for moving his psychotherapy practice online, and had thus far been a success, he said, bemused. He hoped to transition the whole practice to virtual appointments; he would only ever meet new clients online.

Next was Sasha, who offered a shy introduction. American, she was visiting Bali indefinitely. Unlike the other residents who were drawn there by media articles or references from friends, Sasha had not planned her stay. She was petite and soft spoken, and it took some gentle prodding to find out that she sold coconut water back in Colorado, and had just visited her suppliers in Thailand. Just a few years before, she had been working odd jobs in a mountain town, marveling at tourists getting altitude sickness. She knew that the micronutrients in coconut water could help with hydration in challenging climates and started selling it around town. By 2018, her brand of coconut water was distributed in six states and she ran the company online. She said this all casually and with a degree of trepidation, like it was surprising even to her.

"Hi, I'm Jenny Watzka." Jenny was the only person to use a last name, the strong emphasis on the "V" sound betraying her German accent. "I'm from Germany, and I'm an online business coach." Jenny described the death of her father at fifty-seven, and the sudden realization that time was scarce—that her corporate consulting job wasn't the life she wanted for herself. There was no time to wait; Jenny quit her job.

Kash initiated a round of applause—aha moments were staples of a welcome breakfast and introductory conversations, moments of action to be congratulated. Everyone in the coworking space had a moment where they realized that changing how they worked was the fastest way to change how they lived. In my memory, Kash said "Yas, queen!" before Jenny continued. "I quit while on a road trip in Spain and launched my business from the back of the van. I made $40,000 in my first four months."

Jenny was an outlier. Most coworking members were earlier in their work–life transition and in a deliberate stage of exploration to see if they could launch that app, write that book, or work European hours from Asia and retain their job. Many were cost constrained and trying to keep their personal run-rate low, as they dipped into savings to navigate their next steps.

When my turn came, I introduced myself briefly. "I'm Melinda, from Canada. I'm here helping out the Hubud staff. And I'm also doing a master's program that I can work on from here."

The longer version was more complicated. I had visited Hubud four months before, as a tourist. I had tagged on a few days to a business trip to Singapore and Taiwan to visit my friends Renee and Steve, Hubud's owners and cofounders, in Bali. I told them I felt stuck. I knew it was time to get a new job or make some sort of decisive change, but I didn't know what I wanted, and I couldn't see the way forward while living in my "old" life.

During my visit, Renee and Steve told me they were moving to London. After nine years raising their family in Bali, it was their time for a change too. Steve and I went out to dinner, and he suggested that I return to Bali, when I was ready, and be their eyes and ears while the local leadership of Hubud got on their feet. I would be paid a modest stipend, enough to cover my rent and basic expenses. I said yes and came back to Bali carrying my many identities: Steve's eyes and ears, master's student, burnt-out entrepreneur, and worker in transition.

I did not say all this at the welcome breakfast. The simple version— Melinda from Canada—was all I needed.

*

Despite never having worked *for* a coworking space, I had worked *in* many of them. They had helped make a home in cities where I had no friends or colleagues and given me prestige addresses at affordable prices. The most ubiquitous coworking brand was WeWork, an American startup that had quickly grown into one of the largest commercial lessors in the US without buying a single property. WeWork's meteoric ascent was fueled by a wave of technology startups that needed the ability to add "seats" (literally, chairs for people to sit in) quickly. The steady increase of independent contractors and the emergence of long-term business travelers, whose needs weren't met by cafés and Airbnbs, had created many marketing niches for coworking companies.

The only similarity between WeWork and Hubud was the business model. Both had day rates and monthly rates, 24/7 access, communal coffee, and access to printers and other office supplies. The value proposition for a coworking space in Bali was totally different, and it certainly didn't rely on proximity or convenience to just about anything. The Ngurah Rai International Airport, the main airport in Bali, was a two-and-a-half-hour flight from Singapore, and Ubud was another hour or more in local congestion. For North American and European travelers, this amounted to over a full day in transit. But Hubud was never competing with the real-estate model of coworking.

"People told us we were crazy, that coworking spaces were for places like Jakarta—big cities, all over the world—because that was the WeWork model, the real estate play," Renee explained. "We were always making a community play."

Peter, one of the original cofounders, had imagined a space like in *Cheers*, where "everybody knows your name." Renee and Steve, whose backgrounds were in international development and the UN system, imagined changing the way business-as-usual was done. Their shared vision was a space for the parents of Green School children. The Green School, a private school (from pre-K to grade 12) that drew eco-minded families from around the world, was what had attracted each of their families to Bali. The parents would drop their kids off every morning and then go home or to cafés to do their own work. There was no space for them—no space for the parents to make social connections, to build community, to share what they were each working on. Hubud started as a pop-up—a limited-time event at a small, rented space—and validated that even in tropical Bali people enjoyed and *wanted* to work together.

Once Hubud secured a lease and moved into the space on Monkey Forest Road, the membership quickly shifted. Over the first three years, it gradually moved from being long-term expats and Green School parents toward people that looked more like me, single and in their late twenties. Ubud was no stranger to shifting trends and demographics. "Nothing's been the same since *Pray Love Eat*," a cab driver told me, incorrectly referencing the monumentally successful memoir-turned-movie that surged Ubud's tourism in the early aughts.

The volume of spas, yoga retreats, and eco-villages were a testament to Ubud's crowning as a health and wellness destination. But the flood of online workers required different infrastructure, more than just steady internet. Just like the Green School parents, they needed a place to gather, friends to have lunch with, and a sense of connection to others living in Bali at the same time. They needed community.

Before the advent of coworking spaces like Hubud, there had been no way for remote workers, digital nomads, nomads—whatever you want to call them—to find each other beyond chance run-ins or one-off meetups. Once the space opened, it was like a rally cry. Suddenly, a group of people who were *already in Bali*, already working online, could find each other. Collaborate. Bounce ideas off each other and lend and a hand with each other's projects. Once you paid the membership fee, connected to the internet, and attended a welcome breakfast or one of the other 200+ annual events, you were officially in—you were a Hubudian. You belonged.

The vision of a digital nomad utopia in the jungle caught on like wildfire, and soon people were coming to Bali to *be* a digital nomad. There was no talk of work–life balance, only work–life integration. Hubud sold T-shirts with slogans like "post-cubicle survivor" and "our work is changing." Members self-organized workshops and offered each other discounts on products and services. Passion and purpose were as important as profit—and happiness and fulfillment were the ultimate currency. Researchers from Harvard and Oxford sent research teams to observe whatever secret sauce they could bottle to take home. It was clear that Hubud wasn't just selling space—internet and desks—it was selling an aspiration, evangelizing a new way of working and living. And fitting Ubud's reputation for hippie *woo-woo* and alternative therapies, it was selling a path to self-actualization.

Outside of this existential difference, digital nomads were administratively a lot like tourists. Immigration rules prevented foreigners from earning local income (and paying local taxes), unless they had the necessary paperwork. Legally, online workers could work *from* Bali because they weren't working *in* Bali. Some conducted local business in an apparent gray space (sometimes made less gray if the immigration authorities showed up), or if they overstayed their visas, but for the most part, coworking was as innocent as it looked. We were a bunch of predominantly Western people on tourist visas, paying rent to a local business for internet access and a desk. Well, not even a desk. The tables were communal, and first come, first served. Basically, you sat where there was a seat, and if you wanted to leave stuff behind at the end of the day, you could rent a locker.

None of this screamed "office." Held to that standard, Hubud probably would have failed. There was always a broken AC, a clogged toilet. But there was also something appealing about the whole thing. Seductive, even. If you really could work from anywhere, why not in the middle of the jungle in a town more known for chakra realignment than reliable internet? The critical ingredient for this type of coworking wasn't the physical space anyway—it was the people.

Hubud kicked off a wave of coworking spaces in traditionally tourist locations with beautiful environments and moderate costs of living. By 2015, there were coworking spaces in Thai beach towns and throughout Myanmar and Cambodia. By 2018, the coworking chain Selena had ten locations in Costa Rica alone and had branched out into providing accommodations. Any city or town that had a youth hostel and an internet café in 2013, no doubt had a coworking space by 2019, when I finished my tenure at Hubud. By marketing directly to remote workers and *aspirational* digital nomads, Hubud had generated a cult following on social media and was voted the "World's Best Coworking Community" by *Forbes* and *Huffington Post*. Its status as the first and the original coworking space for digital nomads made it a veritable site of pilgrimage, the first destination on a long journey into the remote work lifestyle.

Jenny and I became friends, much in the way one might with a colleague that you ran into on the street or in the office enough times. Jenny was approaching thirty, white, university educated, and had a cosmopolitan quality that signaled her privilege and comfort in new environments. Basically, she reminded me of myself. We could each choose to work and live anywhere we wanted, and at least for now, she had chosen to work online and travel. But while I was considering if I wanted a job, Jenny was selling Jenny. Her product was herself, a new brand of white-collar worker who packaged and marketed their expertise *and* their lifestyle. Jenny worked with clients so they, too, could run a profitable business and still have time to read, work out, and spend afternoons by the pool. I knew I could live like Jenny if I could work like Jenny. Did I want to?

She smiled and nodded when I asked about her transition out of a "normal" job. "My mum was nervous when I told her my plans. What if I failed? I was one hundred percent sure I would be successful," she said.

We were at a "French" café that had just opened on the main street and alone in the restaurant, outnumbered by staff. Her eye contact was almost unsettling because she spoke with so much confidence. "My old company is holding my job for two years. I can always go back. Failure was never an option, but there was really no bad outcome." Unlike many entrepreneurs who start businesses while working a day job, Jenny was all in from the start. It was like she had never paused to consider a downside or a reality where she wasn't immediately successful.

Jenny's routine was to wake up at eight and choose one nonnegotiable task for her workday. A nonnegotiable task was a full piece of work that would move her or a client's business forward, like launching a new sales funnel or producing content for her blog. Her new YouTube channel needed attention, and she was still active within her Facebook community, that then had more than 1,500 members. She'd go to a restaurant for lunch, then spend an hour reading or taking an online course. Then she'd exercise and be at the pool or beach by three in the afternoon, her workday completed. Even talking about her schedule, Jenny sounded like a consultant. "Email is not a task!" she reminded.

Her target clients were already consultants, people who earned upward of $5,000 a month. She helped them automate and scale operations to increase their revenue. Some clients had gone from $5,000 to $20,000 in monthly revenues. She wasn't helping people get started, she was engineering liftoff. Her clients just needed her know-how to get more customers and take their businesses to the next level.

It sounded almost like a pyramid scheme: starting a consulting business to help people run consulting businesses. There had to be something I was missing.

To get started, Jenny had joined a bunch of Facebook groups targeting entrepreneurs. She started commenting on posts and adding value by responding to, commenting on, and participating in group conversations. She wasn't selling a physical good, just timely access to insight and expertise. If she could help a client solve a timely problem, she could charge for it. Demonstrating expertise publicly, through Facebook or Instagram Live, was meaningful business development, like putting food in a mouse trap timed to go off when the prospective client said to themself, "Yes, I also have that problem."

Jenny was trying to get away from trading her time for money. She wanted a package, an "offer" that could scale. Rather than delivering singular counsel to clients, she created an online course. The course would give multiple clients access to her expertise simultaneously, and let them pause, rewind, and repeat, and take things at their own pace. Jenny was selling a recipe that enhanced the chances of starting an online consulting business on the right foot, and people were willing to pay for it, $500 a pop. In the first four days of selling the course, Jenny sold seventeen licenses.

That was her scalable offer, and the hope was that the client would be so happy with the course that they would want to buy her other "product": one-on-one coaching sessions. She called this her flagship program, and it consisted of weekly one-on-one calls and text support on Facebook Messenger or WhatsApp. Through this process, Jenny realized that her services were more consultative than coaching. A coach asks questions but does not suggest answers or tactics. Jenny gave answers—clients paid her to access them. Her time, tools, methods, and processes created meaningful earning potential for her clients. One client had recently paid her $1,000 for a package that resulted in a short-term earnings boost of $8,000. Jenny called this a win-win, a no-brainer.

Before packing up and leaving her last full-time home in London, she had hired a professional stylist and photographer to help her establish her visual brand. Part of what she was selling was the idea that you could be happy, make money, and live wherever and however you wanted—her photos, styling, and visual brand had to communicate that. The stylist taught her to wear bright, primary colors that photograph well and communicate youth and energy. No patterns—they're feminine (and not in a good way) and distracting. She cut six inches off her hair and decided to be photographed with her glasses on. They communicated authority and would be kept for photos even after laser surgery. Jenny didn't seem to mind. "Now I know exactly what to buy, what looks good on me, and how it aligns with my brand."

Jenny's brand was focused and happy, goal-oriented and fun, serious and lighthearted. It married her professional focus to her target lifestyle. Jenny the consultant and Jenny the globe-trotting digital nomad were the same person. Mobility was part of her brand. This of course required a team of virtual assistants (VAs) that did low-level and repetitive tasks for her. Tim Ferriss's *New York Times* bestseller *The 4-Hour Workweek* had popularized outsourcing as a means of freeing time among digital nomads. VAs were easy to come by via online marketplaces and in dedicated Facebook groups, while PayPal and other internet payment providers made it easy to employ someone in another country or continent. Even if Jenny had built her business at home in Germany, it was likely she'd still rely on staff in the Philippines or India. That Jenny's freedom was built on low-cost labor didn't seem to bother anyone.

Jenny lived by the principle of outsourcing what could be outsourced, and, except for Instagram stories and live videos on Facebook, let her assistant do all the social media scheduling. She paid her support staff by project rather than by the hour. She didn't want her VA to leave her because she got better at her job and needed less time to do it. She aligned pricing around value—so long as her VAs were adding value, Jenny didn't mind if it took them half the time. Win–win.

Jenny was emblematic of a certain type of digital nomad. She could do whatever she wanted—she had a master's degree and could find work in any city of her choosing. Why had she left Germany? What would life on the road give her that life in a city—one static city—could not? And was this about the travel or not being "stuck" anywhere, of being able to decide for herself?

I came to understand that, at least for Jenny, her choice to work independently was about forging her own path, without reliance on an office, a manager, and a company. The travel was just a bonus, a momentary convenience. If her goals changed, Jenny would change too—change her customers, change her services, change her work to keep up with her desired lifestyle.

On her last day in Ubud, Jenny went to pick up a macramé dreamcatcher she'd been eyeing for over a week. She held it up and assessed if it would fit into her luggage. Would it be too wide or too heavy? "I can just throw something away if it is, use it as an opportunity to purge," she said. She planned to buy a souvenir in each place she'd live over the next twelve months; the dreamcatcher was destined to go on a gray wall behind her bed. "Eventually, I'm going to want to be based somewhere," she shared. The gray wall and the dreamcatcher belonged to some future apartment, in some unknown city.

CHAPTER 2

LUNCH AND LEARN

Within a few weeks, I realized Hubud was a distilled concentrated version of the collective culture of tourists, travelers, and expats. Meals became a focal point for meeting interesting people outside of the coworking space. At breakfast I met Bridget, a former corporate attorney from Manhattan, with a thick New York accent, gregarious spirit, and none of the mannerisms I expected from a yoga and breath work teacher.

At a vegan café, I overheard a conversation between a husband and wife, who I later came to know as part of the expat team running a not-for-profit foundation. Their conversation was so outrageous that I struggled to not laugh. They were overconfident, saying things that I would never say out loud to anyone—it was on brand for a restaurant whose specialty was vegan lasagna. After I left that dinner and returned to my temporary guesthouse, I ran into eight staff and interns from Hubud having dinner at the warung, a casual restaurant. It felt like the coworking space wasn't so much a contained building, but a community that floated freely around Ubud. The culture existed in and outside; the coworking space was its most distilled form.

The coworking space was my office, my community center, and the apex of my social life. I went there to work, mostly mentoring staff and communicating project progress to the founders. I'd stay into the evenings to attend community events like a members' dinner, see pitches at a Hackathon, or participate in Toastmasters. During the daytime, the most recurrent events were "lunch and learns," peer-to-peer presentations where one member would present their business or area of expertise to whoever showed up. For the most part, presenters didn't have colleagues working in the space that they were showing off for—they were participating purely out of interest or community spirit. Or for sales and business development. I never really knew if I was walking into someone's pitch for their company, a heartfelt TED-style talk about their road to Bali, or something purely tactical to an area of online business. If you were in the space for long enough, you'd inevitably have a community manager suggesting you do a lunch and learn. Many would treat "speaking at Hubud" like a professional accomplishment, almost like being invited to present at an industry conference, but from the inside the lunch and learns were casual—a group of people in a conference room with the blinds drawn (so we could see the projector) and the AC on full blast.

Lunch and learns were event viewing, one of the few fixed-timing things in the coworking space. Sometimes a couple of day passes would be sold for people who wanted to attend the lunch and learn but weren't otherwise subscription members. At quarter to twelve, an intern or community manager booted out folks working from the conference room to do setup, pulled down a screen, set up the projector, and arranged chairs for the number of people expected. The signup sheet at the welcome desk was an imperfect estimate—there were always dropouts and last-minute joiners. A large group would attract a larger group to join, blindly trusting the judgment of their peers. The room could comfortably seat about twelve, but with a speaker at the front and things projected on the screen, there needed to be a bit of a ring around the speaker. This meant people lined the conference table, then there was another ring of chairs, some on rollers wheeled in from the open space. The AC was effective for the first five minutes as people filed in, but warmed with our body heat, many fresh out of the sun of their scooter ride to Hubud, helmets in hand. The irony of sitting in the dark on a bright, clear thirty-degree day was a reminder that this was a workday.

Carole's lunch and learn was among the first I attended. I introduced myself and showed her how to connect her MacBook to the projector and tested her slides. Then I moved to the back of the room and sat on a beat-up wooden chair, phone and notebook open on my lap, and waited for Carole's presentation. There was an awkward, first day of school feeling during these lunch and learns; it was always someone's awkward first day.

Carole and Ally ran a web development agency that specialized in website development and digital branding. The presentation was at the center of their wheelhouse—substantiating the idea that not only did you need a website to do business, you needed a website your target customers could find. "Fourteen thousand websites go online every day. If you're selling something on the internet, it's important to understand why people go to your website, and how to get them there," said Carole, brimming with quiet confidence.

Carole was the developer on the team, and Ally was a graphic designer.

Together their agency had brought countless websites to life for clients. Their chosen platform was WordPress, one of the most common website platforms in the world and among the best for search engine optimization (SEO). "How are you going to do business online if people can't find your site?" she asked the group of about twelve.

They explained that behind every Google search was a set of keywords that helped Google assess how relevant the content on a site was for any given search. Mastering SEO was part of complex puzzle of search ranking and part of the code anyone with a website needed to crack to make sure they could be found. The universality of the topic had attracted many people, and the room was filled to the brim.

Six months earlier, Carole had left her corporate job as a digital marketer in Cambridge, England. When she told her employer she was leaving, they offered her a contract worth twice the money for half the time. The spare time and padded pockets gave her time to launch her online digital marketing company. She and her wife, Ally, worked together to offer branding and web development services to their clients in the UK and Europe.

Carole and Ally could travel the world without coworking spaces, but why would they? For a small subscription fee, they could drop into a self-curated group of people all going through work–life transitions. The coworking space was for anyone in a transition, and that included how they worked. Yes, there were a lot of young people there, but there were many coworkers launching second careers or doing major career pivots.

Being in their mid-thirties made Carole and Ally among the older members of the coworking space. Because they're spouses as well as colleagues, they worked from the villa they rented rather than pay for two memberships. They did, however, buy day passes for community events at Hubub to meet others. "Community and place aren't the same thing anymore," Carole said.

How did it become possible that you could travel the world on your honeymoon while working full time building a business? The form of mobility seemed like a natural extension of computing and online work, but it was also radical to people who assumed that business and work was to be done close to home, and that the activities of work life and home life were separate.

In 1972, a young man by the name of Jack Nilles was working on a communication system for NASA. An engineer and self-described "rocket scientist" and spacecraft designer, Nilles completed most of his work away from government property, outside the NASA offices in Los Angeles, California. When asked to describe working from home, Nilles said he was "telecommuting." At that time, there were no mobile phones, 5G networks, or Wi-Fi—not even dial-up internet. Telecommuting likely involved files brought home from the office, strewn across a desk beside a typewriter, maybe some reference books, and certainly a corded phone. The communication system Nilles was working on would have involved other people, surely, but with the right information, he was able to do it from the comfort of his home. The prefix "tele" means from a distance, like telephone or telescope. Telecommuting was a portmanteau created by Nilles to describe what he was doing—working from a distance.

Nilles described telecommuting as "periodic work out of the principal office, one or more days per week, either at home, a client's site, or in a telework center." In Nilles' definition, the emphasis was "on reduction or elimination of the daily commute to and from the workplace." His 1974 book *The Telecommunications-Transportation Tradeoff* proposed telecommuting as an alternative to transportation.[1] In the early '70s, there was an oil crisis raging—there was a strong motivation to decrease reliance on fossil fuels. His suggestion for working from home would help decrease traffic, ease urban sprawl, and ameliorate the use of non-renewable resources. To Nilles, telecommuting was the environmental choice for the modern workplace, and anyone who teleworked at least one in ten days was a telecommuter.

Teleworking, by contrast, focused on the mobility of information—the ability for a worker to access and participate in work activities from outside the centralized workspace by moving the work to the worker, rather than the worker moving to the work. Teleworking had nothing to do with a commute, it was simply a way of working.

Nilles wasn't just talking about his own work with NASA when he coined the concepts "telecommuting" and "telework," he was paving the way for the movement of workers and employers toward remote work. In running his NASA project out of his home, he demonstrated that with the right scope of work, information, and access to the needed technology, he could do his job out of the office.

As interest grew in the concept of working from home, realtors and builders began marketing spaces specifically for that purpose. Loft developments gained popularity in the late '70s, particularly urban centers such as New York City's SOHO neighborhood. This new "innovative" building type reinvented the age-old concept of the work home and made it trendy for a new generation, gradually replacing the common understanding of a building type that had existed for generations.[2] Other dual use "live/work" spaces like corner stores, workshops, and home offices were not part and parcel of this "new" concept. The concept caught on particularly among the artistic community, who were already accustomed to working in nontraditional spaces. The work home, a space that was designed and *branded* to blend personal and work use, felt new, fresh, and hip. Yet concurrently, office culture became an entrenched part of city life and an aspirational lifestyle among the now swollen middle class of the Western Hemisphere. Office jobs offered superior wages and became a source of aspiration—the corner office was the pinnacle of power in corporate America.

Nilles' vision (or maybe version) of telecommuting predated the internet. It also focused on the office: he envisioned breaking down the corporate head office into satellite offices, where employees could work closer to home when they didn't need to be at headquarters. "Our primary interest, and the greatest impact on traffic and energy consumption, was reducing the commute to work," Nilles said. Saving workers from physical mobility is almost the antithesis of modern remote work, which encourages mobility outside of both the home and the office, to coffee shops, coworking spaces, cottages and otherwise.

Nilles was wrong about some things, but he correctly anticipated what two things would empower the broad adoption of remote work: self-contained work environments and radical improvements in memory storage and transfer. *The Telecommunications-Transportation Tradeoff* says that "either the jobs of (the) employees must be redesigned so that they can still be self-contained at each individual location, or a sufficiently sophisticated telecommunications and information storage system must be developed to allow the information transfer to occur as effectively as if the employees were centrally collocated [*sic*]."

Nilles' and his colleagues' second point, that "sufficiently sophisticated" information storage and transfer must exist, has been realized through the Cloud. Cloud technology allows for the storage of digital goods on remote servers that can be accessed by users outside the office mainframe. This development has meant that less and less information can only be retrieved from within the four walls of an office space—it's made fully remote work technically feasible by removing the physical walls around access to information. These two points now seem prescient.

Until 1990, offices had been the physical place of work, dominated by meetings, fax machines, printers, and tools that were not accessible outside the four walls of an office. Information was exchanged person to person, orally or on paper. Shortly after the fall of the Berlin Wall in late 1989, the internet, as we know it, was born in 1990. The World Wide Web connected workers with email and virtual office tools. And much liked the changed world order after the Cold War, the standoff between the office and the potential of internet-connected devices emerged—a tug of war that would last the better part of thirty years (and my whole lifetime). People were hired and trained to be experts at filing and information management within office spaces, as the pace of digitization increased the velocity of information. Email allowed for near instantaneous communication whether you were sitting next to someone or sending a message from across the country.

Stories of early remote work largely came from big companies and, maybe surprisingly, within the government. The cost of personal computers was still high, and web-browser, Cloud-based tools did not yet exist. The US federal government took the risk to validate the idea that remote work could work well for them and their workforce. As an employer, the government could massively reduce their cost base by shrinking office spaces and could keep cars off the roads during peak commuting hours too. They ran their first study on telecommuting in 1990, which substantiated that remote work was not only increasingly feasible, but that it was highly desirable for workers. Workers were more satisfied with their jobs and felt telecommuting gave them more flexibility to balance their professional commitments with their family lives, hobbies, and other commitments. To be successful, managers had to more clearly allocate tasks and make sure employees had the information they needed at their disposal. This could mean driving home with a stack of files or books for reference, but the movement of these physical goods was worth it in exchange for free time. I remember my mother buying a fax machine to take on a family vacation to Florida in the mid-1990s. She plugged it into the phone and received morning and end-of-day faxes from her workplace and would then bark out stock trades to her assistant by phone. This was remote work, too, even when the tools were rudimentary or haphazard.

Throughout the '90s, computers became cheaper as the internet became more stable in homes and public spaces. Both factors made remote work more affordable—computing and computers were now a part of most desk jobs, and workers did more and more of their core tasks on or with the aid of computing technology. By 1994–1995, big players like

American Express, IBM, and AT&T started to allow their employees to work remotely, usually from their homes. It was too early to quantify the economic impact of remote work in precise terms, but workers enjoyed the flexibility and were able to achieve comparable results. Companies saved money on rent and could effectively extend the workday by not requiring workers to commute. By 1995, all the ingredients of modern remote work were there—people had computers in their home, and those computers had sufficient memory and storage—but work tools designed to be used online (like Internet Explorer) just weren't robust enough yet.

Knowledge work accelerated in the 2000s for two reasons: the internet and mobility devices (Blackberries, smartphones, and laptops). Managing workflows in a digital environment required the invention of new, digital project management tools. Basecamp (originally 37signals), a popular task management software, launched in 1999 with the design goal to empower remote teams. The early 2000s opened the floodgates for such internet-based software, as wireless and broadband rolled out nationally and guaranteed a reliability of service. It was like the building of highways for the internet—remote employees could finally work without ties to a physical location for their Ethernet connection. The bee-bop-boop sounds of dial-up internet became nothing but a bad memory.

What happened in the office during this period? Tasks changed, and what being at work meant changed too. Workers needed less time to do key tasks, but they spent more time in meetings. More workers were able to do more and more of their job online. The office became a place to come to do work—a venue, sometimes for a collaboration, but often to work alone or alongside colleagues.

Even in the early days, most remote workers were deeply exposed to the internet and internet culture. So, it's no surprise that the first remote workers built the tools that let them to work more effectively out of the office. Virtual collaboration tools that emulated the office experience for online workers were rapidly developed and resulted in totally new market categories, like Voice Over Internet Protocol (VOIP). Skype was the first breakout vendor, and for a time, it was synonymous with an internet phone call. Video chat features allowed organizations to maintain face-to-face connections with colleagues who were not located in the office (and individuals could keep in touch with friends and family without paying long distance fees for the first time). VOIP technology also started being used as part of hiring. Now candidates and hiring managers could make first impressions without meeting in person at the office. Services like GoToMeeting pushed the technology even further and allowed employees to "meet" in virtual conference rooms and share files and presentations, in addition to chatting.

Like most technology, the initial use case, the reason a tool or program was built, was to solve a business problem. In 2012, Google launched Google Drive, a place where in-house and remote employees can access documents and give feedback in real time. Slack, a group messaging platform, was initially built as an internal management software for a game development company. "Slack" stands for "searchable log of all conversation and knowledge." Now, it's the operating systems for the modern workday. Since launching in 2013, Slack has grown into a behemoth among startups. It was valued at $27.7 billion in 2020 and is used by everything from small communities to Fortune 500 companies.

Throughout history, workers have pushed the envelope on employment norms and demanded more from their employers via organized labor movements, legislation, and even revolutions. Where the first industrial revolution brought people together into factories, then later into workplaces and offices, the current unraveling of the workplace into groups of workers connected by the internet is a sort of industrial revolution in reverse. We're moving out of centralized workplaces and into homes, cafés, and coworking spaces. And those places are more varied and diverse than even remote work visionary Jack Nilles imagined.

Nilles realized early on that "technology was not the limiting factor in the acceptance of telecommuting." Instead, he said, "organizational—and management—cultural changes" were far more important in the rate of acceptance of telecommuting. Successful remote work depends on more than just strong internet: it incorporates new management structures, collaborative needs, work structures, and work–life balance opportunities than simply replacing a commute.

CHAPTER 3

MONKEY FOREST

I'd been in Bali for six weeks before I started driving a scooter. I was sick of paying taxi fees, of following a one-way street in a car only to double back to get to my destination. The only way to get from my coworking space, Hubud, to my home in Nyuh Kuning was to go around the Monkey Forest. I don't hate monkeys—I just don't like them. I don't like their intelligence and how they know to lunge toward things of value. I don't like their eye contact and their loud, shrill screeches. And I don't like that I am more scared of them than they are of me.

The most direct route from Ubud to Nyuh Kuning, the neighboring village, was through the Monkey Forest. Tourists would often enter it for a photograph near or with the monkeys, which often resulted in the monkeys snatching their sunglasses, snacks, or even their camera. Passersby on the sidewalk outside the entrance were routinely mauled if they were carrying anything at all in a plastic bag—the monkeys knew they were likely to contain food.

The road through the monkeys' home was more like a well-worn path.

It was roughly paved and characterized by dips, big potholes, and sudden turns. On either side of the three-foot wide path was jungle, the type that climbs into the sky covering the sun. At night, the route was lit by a few dim lamps that were mainly concentrated around an underpass. Almost as soon as you exited the road to get on the Monkey Forest path, you dipped into an underpass. Motorists routinely honked before entering because it was too narrow for two scooters to comfortably fit.

Depending on the time of day, there were equal parts pedestrians and motorists. To be on foot was to not drive a scooter, which, in the local environment, immediately meant you're a visitor. Pedestrians were almost always tourists. The town of Ubud was made up of thirteen small villages bordering one another. Ubud, the downtown, was the most well-known. Nyuh Kuning, immediately to the south, just across the Monkey Forest, was where I stayed in a stand-alone, two-story villa. I had the second story to myself, a large studio with a balcony and rainwater shower and direct access to the rooftop. From there, I had an unobstructed view of the village. In the mornings, the cicadas would wake me before the sun. On really magical days, I'd awaken to a gong—a deep, vibrating alarm that marked a birth at the nearby birth center, and for me, a new morning. To exit my villa, I walked through a small garden and at times would see my landlords' moving between their own living quarters and their warung, a small restaurant that faced the street.

On several evening walks home through the Monkey Forest, a friendly Balinese driver would pull over and ask if I wanted a ride into Nyuh Kuning. We would hobble together a friendly interaction in some combination of English and Bahasa, and I would graciously climb on the back of his scooter. If he slowed down at the other side of the forest, I would thank him and continue on foot. If his English was strong enough, he would insist on taking me right to the door of the warung.

Despite the friendly gestures from strangers, the world would open more if I learned to drive a scooter.

So I hired an expert.

I hired the "Bali Scooter Instructor," a kindly man named Musli (pronounced like the cereal), to give me lessons.

I had three hours of instruction for $30. The best part was that his scooter had "beginner" settings. Musli had installed a screw to block the right hand from jacking the speed and the scooter taking off. I couldn't accelerate past a paltry putz, but once I gained some balance, he would unscrew it to let me go faster.

That afternoon, we moved forward, right, left, and around again. We drove circles in a school parking lot before advancing to a loop around the school, entering and exiting from various entrances to practice my turns. Right turns were harder, as they meant having to fight my instinct to pull into the oncoming lane. Traffic moved on the left, and I needed to recode old habits.

As we started down a path, joining a road for the first time, I slowed down. Each pothole scared me. "Don't go too slow," Musli warned. "If you go too slow, you lose your balance."

Going just a bit faster let me steady the wheels, lift my feet, and refocus my eyes and attention on the road ahead. A bit of speed was better than starting and stopping, and more focused than wobbling from side to side. A bit of speed gave me balance, and with that, I could move forward.

Musli gradually unwound the screw to allow me to accelerate like a normal driver, to let me join traffic, and eventually drive myself home, with Musli sitting right behind me. We drove into Ubud, sat in traffic, and went through the Monkey Forest before pulling up at my door in Nyuh Kuning.

A scooter felt like freedom. I could go where I wanted and no longer depended on friends or taxis to get from A to B. This meant that the list of potential Bs elongated—I discovered more alone on my scooter than I ever would have in the back of a car. If I remained on foot, I'd forever be a tourist. If I was on a scooter, I was moving forward. I wasn't planning to leave or to jump back into my old way of life. I was opening to new experiences and to new uncertainty. With no job or commitments, I was opening the door to unexpected paths forward. It was important to keep moving, to not stall out. Moving was the only way to keep balance. Forward.

CHAPTER 4

GOOD GIGS

"Taxi, taxi!"

It was Saturday night in Canggu, a beach town in Southern Bali. Sun-kissed surfers and tourists were migrating from their accommodations to local bars near the beach. There was a traffic jam of taxis and scooters in front of Old Man's, a popular bar where the average age was about twenty-five.

It was the rainy season, which worked to the drivers' advantage. If the weather was clear, one could easily walk twenty meters and find another driver offering a ride for the same price. A driver was one of the most common occupations in Bali, where the economy was 80 percent services for tourists. The drivers would keep yelling, even walking or driving beside you, until you expressed a desire to negotiate or said a firm no.

"How much you pay?" the driver asked as I walked by. I didn't start the conversation, but my lack of scooter gave me away as someone in need of a ride.

Several cars were sitting idle. Despite the prevalence of professional drivers, over 150 tourists lose their lives to accidents each year. The cost was only between two and ten dollars per day to rent a motorbike, and many vendors didn't require ID or a valid license. Tonight, you could see the drunk drivers swerving through the streets. Vehicles drove on the left side of the road, in the British tradition, but after a few Bintang beers, many foreign drivers started to veer right.

My silent negotiation tactic worked, and the driver lowered his price by 75 percent. Soon the car was moving faster than scooters, passing on the right—almost into ongoing traffic. The rules of the road here were all custom, not law. If someone snuck in front of you, you deferred and let them go ahead. Traffic kept moving.

"She's going to die," the taxi driver said with a laugh as we sped through an intersection. There was a blond, Caucasian woman on a scooter ahead of us. She wasn't wearing a helmet and lacked the confidence of a seasoned driver. "It's always the skinny ones first."

During the day, families would fit two adults and two children on a scooter; you'd often see kids as young as ten driving unaccompanied.

Navigating by foot was burdensome. Not because it was 30 degrees Celsius and humid, but because the roads simply weren't designed to be walkable. There were holes in the ground that could swallow a toddler. Some were covered with metal plates with the logo of the Regency, the local equivalent of state or province, but they were only recently installed. For months there had been large, one-meter-deep holes every few meters on the sidewalks, which meant you had to be able and willing to jump in and out of the street to walk anywhere. Some sidewalks had bump lines down the middle, so that the visually impaired could feel which side of the sidewalk was theirs. The law of the road may have been to stick to the left, but the sidewalk was a confusing free-for-all. It was much easier to drive.

We pulled up to a guesthouse, hidden within a family compound; I paid the fare (under two dollars) and got out.

*

Drivers are a type of deskless worker, meaning their work is not done sitting at a desk. Google estimates that 80 percent of the global work-force is deskless, and to varying degrees, relies on being in a specific location to deliver their goods and services. The proportion of deskless workers is higher in countries like Indonesia that have less developed knowledge sectors—fewer desk jobs. Remote workers are predominantly knowledge-workers. Even the term "desk workers" seems to imply the presumed relationship between knowledge work and offices. Now that both offices and computers are mobile, the term doesn't suit anymore.

Technology is changing the mobility and "work" of all industries, including driving. Ride-hailing services like Uber and Lyft led the tech transition for deskless workers. The first time I used Lyft, in 2013 San Francisco, a Toyota Prius with a fuzzy pink mustache on the bumper, pulled up, and the driver gave me a first bump to welcome me to the car. I remember taking a taxi the same week, walking against traffic until an available driver drove by and I anxiously hailed him down. By comparison, Lyft felt like a dream, albeit a quirky one.

Lyft and Uber have been focal points of the transition toward the gig economy. The gig economy is comprised of one-off jobs like rides or odd household tasks—deskless jobs—that can often be found on apps or websites. Gig economy jobs offer no guaranteed hourly or monthly wages and shift responsibility for income from the company to the individual. Ride-hailing apps let anyone become a driver and skirt regulations that previously protected taxi drivers from oversupply. In San Francisco, New York, Toronto, Paris, and other global cities, there were protests, often led by taxi drivers, looking to ban ride-hailing apps. The suicides of a several New York City taxi drivers were attributed to the stress of loosening taxi regulations that dramatically devaluated their prized, regulated medallions.

San Francisco was ground zero—where the technology behind Uber and Lyft was built—and where users started using the services en masse. The venture capital industry dumped more and more money to lure riders between the two competitors, often in the form of subsidizing rides. The companies have also expanded the "on demand" economy to delivering food and allowing for carpooling. All this was happening while more Uber and Lyft drivers slept in grocery store parking lots, totally priced out of buying or renting local real estate. For all the "success" of the ride-hailing industry, you have to question who is in the driver's seat—drivers, riders, or the companies building the technology?

Hailing a ride has never been a problem in Bali. But the potential for tech to create efficiency by matching drivers with riders and predetermining pricing (without negotiation) was too good an opportunity to miss. Locally, the dominant ride-hailing apps are GoJek and Grab. GoJek is the scooter equivalent of Uber. You match with a driver who will put you on the back of their scooter and drive you as far as thirty-five kilometers. You can pay with cash or with GoPay and receive a discount. There's GoJek for scooters, GoCar for cars, and GoFood for food delivery. For a fee, GoJek will even go shopping for you and deliver.

The founders of GoJek and Grab are both Indonesian graduates of Harvard Business School. They were inspired to replicate Uber's success in North America and now compete to dominate the ride-hailing economy in Southeast Asia.

"How is GoJek here?" I asked the waiter. I was in a Mexican restaurant in Canggu and looking to return to Ubud. All the drivers I was in contact with were in Ubud, so my choices were negotiating on the street or using Grab or GoJek to get a car home.

"You shouldn't have a problem," he said. "I'm a GoJek [driver] every day, there should be plenty of cars." The prices on Grab and GoJek were about one-fifth of what you'd find on the street, undercutting drivers who'd sit and wait for potential customers. GoJek drivers made up for in volume what they would otherwise lose in price. But the savvy drivers of Bali used the chat features within the app to ask for more money. It was common to match and chat with several GoJek drivers before finding one that was willing to accept the GoJek price and meet you within a reasonable time frame. Unlike in a major city like New York or San Francisco, where the drivers were circling the city waiting for a new match, many Bali drivers just stayed at home and waited—they only stepped into a car when someone matched on the app.

"Don't you live in Canggu?" I asked. If he lived locally, there would be no reason for him to know the volume of GoJek traffic leaving the city.

"No, I live in Denpasar," the waiter replied. Denpasar was about an hour north of Canggu and the city nearest Bali's main airport. Minimum wage in Bali was about $350 USD a month. It was more affordable to commute to jobs in the touristy beach towns like Canggu than to rent a room locally. Renting a sparsely decorated room to an Indonesian would net about $100 per month. But if you could make a place nice enough to list on Airbnb, you could enjoy a significant markup—foreigners would pay about $25 per night. Unable to afford this, the waiter subsidized his commute by bringing a passenger along with him on the ride to and from work.

The road between Canggu and Denpasar was well trafficked, but not built for it. There was no separation between the road and commercial and residential properties. Kids played on the shoulder beside busy traffic. It wasn't a real highway, and it showed. It could take up to an hour and a half to drive the fourteen kilometers.

The local taxi drivers were not interested in participating in the ride-hailing gig economy. Driving was their whole livelihood—not a way to subsidize a commute. These drivers would chase GoJek and Grab drivers to their homes and damage their cars—a primary economic asset—as retribution for their attack on the way things have been. The airport was littered with protest signs, so you knew directly upon arrival that to use a mobile app was to forsake the local economy.

My GoJek taxi was an unmarked car. When we arrived to my village, the driver slowed down. There was often a traffic cop sitting at the only entrance to the village to make sure no GoJeks or Grabs stole business from the local drivers. Since I lived there and the car didn't have a GoJek sticker, the driver agreed to enter. I only came to understand these dynamics long after I paid my fare and was safely home.

*

Most conversations on the gig economy focus on its impact of the deskless workforce, but the trend toward independent work is also alive and well within the knowledge economy. The online gig economy for knowledge work is replacing some of the work that once thrived within agencies and consulting firms. Want a quick graphic design? No need for a full-time designer, you can hire someone on a marketplace like Fiverr for, well, a fiver. Many platforms allow you as the buyer to name your price and receive competitive offers from workers around the world. These online marketplaces of talent provide visibility and access to services at lower rates, as well as the ability to pay for or offer piecemeal work for people who have a very specific skill set that they can do online with low effort. These marketplaces offer a great way to earn income, comparable to that which they might achieve in a more typical job with the added flexibility being a contractor or self-employed.

For people in the creative professions, piecemeal work can help build a portfolio and get a foot in the door in more established parts of the industry. Rather than pursuing entry-level, full-time roles, many are building themselves a portfolio of diverse work experiences that allow them to land in more lucrative or formalized environments. The gig economy has become the cost of entry to more stable jobs and employment.

The coworking space skewed foreign, at a scale of four to one, at times, more. Indonesian members (and foreigners with working papers) got a discount (to account for purchasing power), but they were otherwise just like other members of the community. It was all too easy not to notice the power dynamic at work within the coworking space and outside of it. Foreigners were welcome customers, treated like VIPs by the Balinese and other Indonesians. The power dynamic was thinly veiled in client/customer language but hidden in plain view. Foreigners working from Bali were typically earning a foreign wage, pegged to the cost of living or economic conditions of wherever "home" was. Indonesian labor standards were much cheaper and primarily earned through service.

My "cheap" meals and "affordable" housing reflected the segmentation of opportunity and the privilege afforded me as a Westerner versus an equally talented Indonesian, who would get paid a fraction of the amount for the same services rendered. If roles were reversed, I would be infuriated. But I never thought to be; it was the way things were, and the structural inequity had been so internalized that I and many others would marvel at how well we could live on our American salaries while living in Indonesia and spending rupiah.

These economic realities became clearer by making friends with Indonesians. And that's where Monica came in. Monica was everywhere at Hubud. She was the stereotypical gossip monger, connector, busybody, and social butterfly.

Monica grew up on Java, Indonesia's largest island and home of Jakarta, the capital and most populous city. After briefly studying abroad in Germany, she moved to Bali to start a wedding planning business. Jakarta was too urban and not a wedding destination—Bali felt better aligned with her goals. A lot of economically mobile Javanese work in Bali, much like people move around within other large countries. Outside of being a prime wedding destination, moving to Bali allowed Monica to be more independent from her large family, to continue to speak Bahasa Indonesia, and to meet more potential international clients.

Monica's business was going well until the volcanoes erupted in 2017. Mount Agung erupted five times and filled the sky with ash, with over three hundred flights and 27,000 passengers were impacted by the eruptions. Clients started canceling their weddings on Bali, and Monica's terms of service didn't include natural and environmental disaster. She had to refund all their deposits in addition to losing the revenue. All entrepreneurs learn some lessons the hard way, and the cancellations were enough to sink Monica's business.

Even without an official wedding planning business, friends often joked that Monica did her own lead generation by actively introducing singles. She was constantly connecting new members and keeping track of "fresh faces" in the space. (Many found it unsurprising that Monica's immediate family purportedly worked in military intelligence.) She knew everything about everyone, and she was the first person members called in an emergency. The contradiction of us living there and driving up prices for Indonesians like her, while also providing the clientele for her wedding planning business or future ventures felt odd to me. She was one of the few Indonesians I met outside of a service context.

CHAPTER 5

LOCATION INDEPENDENT

It was Friday night in Ubud, and the coworking space was clearing out. Within a few hours it would be packed to the brim again for beer pong, a drinking game popular on college campuses where teams of two paired off against one another. Both winning and losing involved drinking beer out of full, big, red Solo cups. Teams were listed on a chalkboard, with small flags drawn beside their names. I counted seven different nationalities among the fifteen teams vying for the title that night. Rihanna and Michael Jackson played on booming speakers. The vibe was very "American college party."

Rob paced in front of a makeshift beer pong table, running his fingers through his grown-out hair. He had been traveling for months with a few friends from England and wanted some dedicated time to spend on a personal project—a new phone-based party game. He teamed up with Dan, a long-term digital nomad who spent his time building and selling web addresses (URLs). Dan wrote posts and built traffic through SEO so more people could find him on Google. Once there were a significant number of monthly visitors, he sold the URLs at a profit.

Dan had been in the coworking space for months, and he and Rob laughed like old friends. Massimo slapped Rob's shoulder when they missed a shot. Rob didn't know Massimo's name until that afternoon, when he stopped by Rob's desk to ask about visiting a massage parlor together. The two left for an hour, had back and head rubs at a nearby day spa, and returned in time for beer pong. People interacted like old friends, but many had only known each other for just a few days. There was a quick bond of being in the same place, at the same time, similar to making friends while backpacking. We were all working in the same way—alone, but open to new experiences.

There was no awkward mingling. The beer pong was observed like a sport, with non-players cheering from the sidelines. The average age had dwindled and was now firmly in the mid-twenties. For me, it was like it was a reenactment of a time I'd thought I'd left behind; for others, this was their college experience—they were literally in their college years and studying abroad, interning at Hubud. The staff were totally indiscernible from the coworking members, who'd each paid a nominal fee to cover the cost of supplies (beer) that evening.

Any confusion I had between this being my workplace and being my social life went out the window when I arrived. I grabbed a beer, made some new friends, and walked home at the end of the night.

*

My social circle in Bali was different than it had been anywhere else. How I spent my time, who I spent it with, and what I started to aspire to started to change. Within weeks I had bought *Designing Your Life* at a local bookstore and reread *The 4-Hour Workweek* after I found it within a sharing library at Hubud. I began scheduling self-care at a local spa and bought a yoga pass to a local studio. I started letting myself take personal time on weekdays and would do some writing or admin work on weekend mornings if I felt like it. There wasn't more work in my life, but there was more life in my work. I felt like I was living the life of one of the motivational T-shirts sold in the lobby. Time began to move at my pace, rather than me moving at the pace of an employer. I wasn't without stress or obligation, but I was told that my relationship to the work mattered, and that what I brought to the work was a part of the quality of work I could deliver. I'd drank the Kool-Aid.

I'd started leaving my computer in my locker at the coworking space (knowing that the lock and 24/7 security would keep it safe) and returned on a Saturday morning to work on some writing. The Saturday morning crowd was different than Friday's beer pong. All evidence of the debauchery was gone, and the patio had returned to its tranquil state. Unlike usual, I sat in the heart of the coworking space on the main floor, on a bench facing a long table. I sat there cross-legged facing a fan, plugged in my computer and got to typing. After an hour and a half, I had done the work I'd set out to and walked my now-empty coffee cup to the sink.

Standing at the bar table opposite the sink were Erik and Ethan. After nearly a month working in the space, it felt like running into mutual friends I'd heard about but never actually met. Ethan and Erik were cool, popular, tall, blond, and handsome.

Ethan had the sort of easy familiarity with his surroundings in the coworking space that made me think he'd have that same sort of confidence in most any space. He had a yoga practice and was vegan—he didn't even drink iced water (he said it stressed the body), and spoke openly about spirituality. He would often drive to the beach to play ultimate Frisbee. Ubud was made for people like Ethan. He, I thought, was what a digital nomad looks like.

As I packed up and prepared to leave, Erik, an intern from Denmark, greeted me near the watercooler, and we fell into an easy conversation. Erik introduced me to Ethan in his friendly way, with a smile across his face the whole time. I'd made assumptions about Ethan that surprised me when he asked my plans for the day and struck up conversation.

Ethan's girlfriend was visiting, so he wanted to get in a few hours of work before continuing with his day. "I love this space. It's the perfect balance of social and get work done," Ethan said. "I like to feel like I'm out in nature, and the bamboo makes it so clear that this isn't a typical office space. I tried other workspaces, but I would say hello, and the people would just wave 'hi' and go back to looking at their computers."

Hubud was explicitly social and collaborative. People shared their time and skills freely. It was meant to feel social, but the crowd on Saturday morning was there for the physical space, not the social atmosphere. It was just more productive than working from home.

"Sometimes I think that people use coworking spaces to see other people working," said Erik. "Working alone is tiresome, but here, there's always someone to take a break with or ask a question to. There's also people working alone in the quiet space, and you can be alone together if you want to."

We were all there, both in Bali and at the coworking space, for different reasons. Despite what many believed, myself included, digital nomads or foreigners working from vacation destinations didn't share demographics. There were commonalities, mostly around liberal social values—an important subcultural value, to be sure—but the motivations were all over the place.

Ethan worked for an American nonprofit that was doing a local pilot. He came to Bali within a week of meeting the company's director. Ethan went where the work took him—and didn't look back. He was there for the opportunity that best aligned with his professional interests, that happened to lend itself to a particular lifestyle.

Erik was at Hubud as an intern as part of his post-secondary education in Denmark, and the spirit of the place was rubbing off on him. He started to experiment with business ideas that could allow him to live in Bali, or wherever, for longer periods. "I don't see the benefit of having firm work hours," he said. "Business and pleasure can go together. If I want to manage my time, why shouldn't I?"

For Alexis, life on the road wasn't a glamorous decision—it said more about her home community than her desire to live a life on the road. She graduated from theater school in Canada and was one of her only classmates to get a full-time job immediately after graduation. Minimum wage was close to eight dollars at the time, and Sam's job paid her thirteen. Decent money, she thought. But the thirteen dollars in daily transit fares and three hours spent commuting made work feel tiresome. She counted it up, and every cent she made was going to rent, phone and internet (not even cable TV), and food. She could only make minimum payments on her student loans, and a night out with a friend would have to go on her credit card. She did this for a year and then was offered a job with the circus. She literally joined the circus and traveled for two and a half years. She was able to save more money on the road with the circus subsidizing her travel and cost of living in cities around the world. When she returned to Toronto, she started taking contracts with her former employer for a month or two at a time. They wouldn't agree to let her work remotely but kept hiring her back seasonally. Even with a full-time job, Toronto wasn't working for her. She knew that she couldn't afford to do entry-level work, so she left.

To Alexis, it looked like it was easier to be a digital nomad than find entry-level work that paid enough to live in a Western city.

Alexis was able to live and work anywhere ten months a year, returning to Canada for regular seasonal work for the other two months. She preferred extended stays in places where she had existing groups of friends and she could afford a more comfortable lifestyle. Hubud was her "home" coworking space in Bali because she felt less stigmatized for having an employer, rather than in spaces that were explicitly geared toward entrepreneurs.

"Our generation has a different perspective on what work is. Part of the reason I work like this is because I want a work–life balance. In Toronto, I'd be putting myself into debt to go for a beer. Here, I can have a nice breakfast, work for a couple hours, go to yoga class, then go out to dinner—and I can afford it," she explained. For her, the quality of life in a place like Bali was beyond what she could reasonably afford in an expensive big city. "I'm not willing to work eighty hours a week and not have a life, just to make money."

For Alexis and many others, remote work was a solution to a problem. The problem: purchasing power. Their dollar didn't go far enough in the places they lived, and they felt their best option was to get out. Sure, they could stay and work to increase their wages and achieve some form of economic mobility, but the short-term tradeoffs, with no promise of future progression, weren't enough. It was faster to go outside the system and earn the same wage, while living in a lower-cost environment. Paired with the explorer lifestyle, dynamic social scenes, and variety, it was easy to convince oneself that being a digital nomad was actually a lifestyle to aspire to, rather than one that was pursued because of isolation or economic stagnation somewhere else.

The increasing accessibility of global travel and the *fun* aspect of it seemed like an obvious first place to start. An easy first reason why some would be attracted to the digital nomad lifestyle. And that was certainly the case for some, but for others, the sense of stagnation was unstuck through extraction—leaving their home city or country. In this context, their preference for living in Bali or wherever felt rational: If you could make the same wage, living in Thailand as you could in Toronto or New York City, why would you choose to be there when that wage went so much further in Bali? Alexis wasn't the only one who asked herself this fresh out of university, when it was as good a time as any to travel the world.

I met Beth, who was in Bali working as a virtual assistant. After landing a few steady clients, she also became a digital nomad. She had more work than she could handle herself and ended up subcontracting to others, eventually starting an online agency for VAs.

Here again, the problems and the solutions were confounded for digital nomads. Was this group entrepreneurial because they wanted to be? Or were they digital nomads because they could take chances and become entrepreneurial by living in lower-cost environments, knowing that their basic needs were satisfied? Were these people really location independent or just economically stagnant within their home communities? Living abroad allowed many to explore interests, business models, ways of working, and ways of being in the world that were too difficult to do at home, where fixed costs were high and cultural conformity mattered. Relationships were built upon existing identities that made it difficult to try on or integrate new ones being on the road. Being part of a mobile community of people seeking something new made it easier to try on new hats, to develop new friendships in new ways, and to control costs while experimenting. It was easier to preserve whatever nest egg would allow for someone to reenter their old life—or to set up a new one. And it was easier to take risks, knowing the biggest cost incurred was time spent traveling. That's why the spirit was one of hopefulness and not isolation. That's how a group of people, these nomads, knew that there was something they could find through their mobility and working remotely that they couldn't find working at home.

CHAPTER 6

YOGA CHURCH

"Breathe into your corners, start to feel the edges of your body," Meghan said as she walked toward the front of the yoga studio. "It takes time, but it manifests in how you speak, how you move, and who you are."

We were at Yoga Church, a weekly Sunday morning yoga class. The room was filled with long, lean people in matching patterned Lycra pants. We were all here to breathe into our corners, to find the edges of who we were.

"Turn to the three people you don't know and muffin your body onto theirs," Meghan announced. She demonstrated that this meant having bodies make full contact with each other and then holding on. She was not looking for quick, double-back-pat kind of hugs.

People start turning and introducing themselves before giving full contact hugs. After enough time has passed for three exceedingly long, sticky hugs, Meghan invited everyone to return to their mats and to find a comfortable sitting position. For some this meant sitting cross-legged, while many opted to sit on their heels. If neither was comfortable, there were yoga blocks meant to help with body alignment and comfort.

"Can you just be here without agenda?" Meghan asked.

Meghan led the class through a series of poses, readings, and instructions aimed to enhance the practice of yoga and the connection between body and mind. Her readings weren't religious but rather focused on command of self. She believed breath and movement were ways to connect with our highest selves, to vibrate at our highest frequencies. Over sixty people flooded the room to be near her. Meghan was a bit of a celebrity—with over 150,000 Instagram followers. She taught yoga and trained teachers around the world.

Meghan shared that she found yoga in a time of personal struggle. She trained to teach and felt it was her calling—it was the best way for her to share her wisdom with the world. She was also about to release her own line of yoga clothing that was ethically made, dyed, and sold in the shop just outside. When one's consciousness was elevated, sustainable behavior spilled into the way you acted, what you bought, and how you consumed.

Meghan cued very gently, each step an invitation to move and breathe. She was thoroughly likable and gave herself time to laugh.

The class was called Yoga Church, but Meghan made it clear that the higher power she was referencing was one's self and the ability to harness one's own attention and focus.

"We do inner work because it manifests externally," she said. Unlike a lot of American classes that better resemble cardio aerobics, there was no rush. Meghan encouraged everyone to pursue their practice at their own speed.

"Lean into your threshold. It's the point where your body pushes back on you. It feels uncomfortable, but it's where your inner power lays."

Two and a half hours later the class ended, and participants gradually filed out of the room. A few minutes later, several of us were eating brunch at the same nearby restaurant.

CHAPTER 7

HETEROTOPIA

"A-tero-topia," said Giulia, as we sat in the Denpasar airport. "Airports are a classic heterotopia."

Giulia was en route to Melbourne, Australia, to start a PhD in urban geography with a focus on coworking spaces. I was on a visa run, exiting and reentering the country to start a new tourist visa. Giulia spoke with her hands and face, and had a distinct and charming Italian accent. "Do you know heterotopia?"

The airport didn't feel like Bali, we said. It was like we had already entered another world, with its own rules and norms. Heterotopias were first described by philosopher Michel Foucault as "other" spaces—worlds within worlds. They mirror but also contradict what exists outside of them. They exist outside the world we know and create their own norms and values. Foucault described the concept of heterotopia as it relates to places like cemeteries, prisons, and fairs. Now there are many more heterotopias. The airport we were sitting in was certainly one of them.

"I'm really interested in the semiotics of spaces," she continued. "If we were in a mall, and they kept announcing which store was closing, we would hate the mall; but in an airport, it's totally normal to hear announcements interjecting on a loudspeaker. Every heterotopia has its own signs and signals and its own norms to uphold."

She had become fascinated by these "other spaces," in her case, coworking spaces, and how they shaped communities. While living in Bali, Giulia made her income doing freelance writing contracts and some journalism. Previously she earned two master's degrees from prestige universities in London and China, and then switched modes entirely and worked on a luxury boat. Hers was the sort of vast, sprawling intelligence that felt displaced in the workforce.

As we approached our gates, we gave each other a big hug. It was the sort of goodbye that felt like a "see you later," because it was so normal to see each other on a daily or weekly basis. But the emotional space between me and Giulia was cavernous. She was saying goodbye to two years of adventure and self-discovery, on her way to start a funded PhD in Australia, while I would return to the "Island of the Gods" in thirty-six hours.

I wasn't the only one coming and going on visa runs or seasonally. Many foreigners left for the rainy season, migrating to Thailand or Vietnam. I left to meet my family for Christmas. But once back on the island, it felt like time hadn't passed, that the through line was life in Bali and not the goings on or the life I led elsewhere in the world, at "home," wherever that was now. Everything felt as permanent as an anchor in water, heavy to lift and quick to settle. Was I unmoored or trying a new harbor? It felt like I'd been there for a lifetime.

Grace had recently returned to Bali after two months in Chang Mai, Thailand. The start of Thai smoke season coincided with the end of Bali's rainy season. So, she packed up her carry-on and booked a flight back to Bali. The carry-on life is a stark contrast to the environment she was raised in, which prized material goods. Her parents left China for Hong Kong, and later the United States, settling in the New York City area when Grace was a child. They never threw anything away. Even if all the stuff was unneeded, it was proof that that family had made it out of poverty. There were boxes and boxes of unused items. There was no scarcity. This was their American dream.

Now at thirty, Grace was in the process of reorganizing her life around her own values—and that included investing in experiences over things. Before first arriving in Bali about nine months before, Grace achieved success by almost any parent's marker. She finished high school and was admitted to Harvard, where she studied psychology and dramatic arts. She took marketing jobs, first in New York, then in the San Francisco Bay Area. By any metric, Grace was successful—the type of child any parent would be proud of.

And then she quit.

Burned out from the grind of excelling at fulfilling the expectations of others, Grace packed her things and hit the road. With a prestigious education and access to professional opportunities wherever she chose to go, Grace could find work wherever she wanted. When I met her, she had traveled through thirty-eight countries and was making her living as a life and business coach.

Grace's parents wanted her life to be stable. "My dad would love it if

I worked at, like, Goldman Sachs," Grace said one afternoon as we sat on the bench adjacent my home swimming pool, widening her eyes at the words "Goldman Sachs" as if to emphasize how far from her father's dream job she has drifted. "Their biggest fear is poverty."

Taking a high-flying corporate job was standard for Ivy League grads, who flocked to finance and management consulting in droves after graduation. William Deresiewicz, a graduate of Columbia and a former professor at Yale, calls these students "excellent sheep." His bestselling book by that title traces the idea that rather than creating free thinkers, elite American colleges encourage conformity toward the ideals of capitalism, often in the form of taking jobs at places like Goldman Sachs. Over 50 percent of Ivy League graduates end up in management consulting or finance immediately after graduation.[3]

"So, for my parents, especially because they worked in sweatshops for twenty years trying to make it, I am the validation. As soon as I got into Harvard they were like, 'we made it, we're fine,'" Grace said.

What also came with the Harvard degree was the expectation to earn money—lots of it. "My mum said, 'she's going to make so much money!'"

They just didn't understand why she wouldn't use all her newfound privileges to take a conventional route to a conventional job. "They're always saying, 'Grace, the world is your oyster.'" Grace's dad was never able to go to college or even finish high school. Like the children of many immigrants to the United States, education, particularly a college education, was the ultimate sign of success. "Social status is also a big thing, but they have it through my education."

Parental expectations are one of the things that many young location independent professionals buck, often foregoing big salaries and their parents' definition of success for more modest living but greater adventure through travel.

Grace was calm and gentle, and so was the language she used. She used her hands in big, round motions either toward or away from her body rather than speeding or raising her voice when she was excited. She made elongated eye contact and would widen her eyes in interest to a response. She studied drama, but her way of being in the world seemed more than a dramatic flair. She made people, even in social settings, feel heard and appreciated. She talked about values and didn't "hold space" (another of her favorite sayings) for small talk.

Grace didn't expect to be coaching forever, but she did expect that coaching would be a part of her next professional role. She envisioned returning to the US in less than a year, where she'd probably work in a tech company. She described this shift with the same somber, deeply felt understanding that she described coaching. "One of the recent shifts I've had is I'll get this all out of my system, then I'll settle down. And I think my most recent shift is that I can see myself really loving splitting my time between San Francisco and Lisbon or somewhere like that." Somewhere transient, relatively affordably, and cultured. Somewhere that has other people like Grace.

Many people use physical mobility to create big shifts in their life, and to use that time to create a vision of life when they "reenter" or return to somewhere, wherever that may be. When Grace reentered life in the US, it would be after almost two years of travel and coaching, and she thought she'd be ready by then. Now in her thirties, her considerations were moving toward making a family of her own and supporting her parents in their retirement. "In fifteen years, I expect to be in the Bay Area, maybe in Oakland, with a partner and kids. When I envision a semi-perfect life or an ideal lifestyle, maybe ten years into the future, I'd like to have kids." She told me that she planned to live in a house that they could rent out when they would travel for months at a time, maybe even having two houses and renting the one that's not occupied. "I imagine coaching being an income stream I can turn on and off, and just restart. That's something I can build in the next few years."

This vision of the future sounded idyllic and was not uncommon among digital nomads. Many digital nomads would acknowledge that they wouldn't travel as a lifestyle forever, but few described wanting to be in one place all year. The idea of a seasonal lifestyle, of having one foot in two places, seemed extremely appealing. This was feasible if both places either had low costs of living or an accessible real estate market. It would be hard to be seasonal in some expensive cities, say New York City, without being wealthy enough to either carry an apartment all year or being able to rent it out (at nearly double monthly rents) via platforms like Airbnb. But as I heard Grace speak, what separated us wasn't professional skills, education, or experience—it was her confidence. Could I do that too? Could I live in one place, travel regularly to others, and bring my work with me? What separated us was our desire or momentary willingness to work independently. If I wanted to join a team and live this way, my only way forward was a remote-first job (or starting a business). Like many big changes, the future of work starts at the individual level, with people making rational choices for their own self-interests, and everything else moves toward them. More people wanted to work online than there were remote-friendly jobs; not everyone would start a business to have the privilege. As I prepared to leave Bali, I thought that more people would choose to work online and live in whatever community appealed to them for social, economic, or cultural reasons—if they only had the opportunity to work remotely.

CHAPTER 8

GETTING TO WORK

I didn't think an office job was what I wanted—until it was. After seven years working independently and on remote teams, I decided the time was right for me to look for what my family and peers would recognize as a "normal" job.

When I thought about what I wanted from my work life, or from the next step in my career, I thought about working in a team environment with colleagues and collaborators. Most of the jobs that fit that description would be in an office, which narrowed my search to a few cities that I wanted to live in. And that meant I'd become an office worker. I was used to living around digital nomads and people who prized the alignment of lifestyle and work, and independence and mobility, but there weren't yet enough jobs that were remote-first to make a remote-only job search practical. I found a job I was genuinely interested in via a tweet—it was the only job I'd applied for. I sent in a CV (that was it) and had a screening call with the hiring manager. I was forthright about where I was in life and what I was looking for, and thought that if they hired me, I was going in with eyes open to what the job would mean to my lifestyle. I was willing to make the tradeoffs if they meant the chance for more structured, on-the-job learning and professional development. I wasn't the perfect candidate, but I applied anyway—I'd read once that women are more self-selective in applying for roles when they don't check every box, and I was silently determined to shoot my shot. I sent in the application and was asked to interview.

On the morning of my interviews, I met Richard, a British friend from Hubud, at my favorite vegan restaurant for breakfast and interview prep. I'd received some briefing materials twenty-four hours prior to the interview, which with the time change meant they'd arrived when I was long asleep. I read them over in the morning and showed up to breakfast with a notepad and a bit of anxiety. Most of the experience I'd had in Bali had been about opening up myself to different ways of knowing, and of challenging assumptions about how I wanted to live and work. Late that night I'd be thrown into a video conference with a traditional corporation ten thousand miles away and be expected to give well-structured answers to questions I hadn't considered in months. Richard helped me gain access to the parts of myself that knew the answers, that knew the approach I wanted to take, but that needed some prodding and some permission to turn back on after months of dormancy. He coached me.

What was the appeal? I wanted stability. I wanted to engage a part of my skills that hadn't been developed working from the jungle. I wanted something where progress looked more clear-cut and visible, something where there was a path in front of me to follow and I wouldn't have to spend so much energy figuring it out. I wanted the opportunity to specialize a bit—working independently made me aware of just how generalized a lot of my skills were. Everyone was selling something different, but the methods of making a website, creating a value proposition, figuring out how to talk about it and how to find customers—those tactics were universal. I wanted to be able to dig into something without being a one-woman shop.

My key insight was that it didn't need to be forever. I was stereotypically millennial and knew it was as normal to switch jobs as to get a promotion. In my mind, it was a two- or three-year commitment, max. I could do anything for a year. I could try anything for a year.

That evening starting at 10:30 p.m. local time, there were three interviews that I took from an empty Hubud. During the interview, they were selling themselves to me as much as I was selling myself to them.

I slipped into a mentality I hadn't existed in for a while—wondering what to wear, worrying about being precisely on time, and feeling that everything needed to go just right. I had become more casual and easygoing while working in Bali, and was more tuned into my emotional state and that of others. In switching back into "work" mode, I realized just how much this type of work, this way of living, had changed me. I knew that getting or not getting the job, whatever I did next would be impermanent—that I could change my mind again later. If this was the stepping stone or not, it was worth having a conversation to assess fit, in both directions, rather than jumping to conclusions and assuming that just because I'd never had a "normal" office job that I wouldn't like it. I'd become more open-minded to the deeply conventional.

Flying to North America for the interview was both challenging and impractical—twenty-four hours in transit plus the jetlag would make it difficult to perform while on site. And the cost of the trip, in time, energy, and money made doing it by video the smart choice. But because remote interviews weren't part of the normal process, there wasn't a playbook for how to do it. They just did the same interviews with the same process online, transposing what they would have done in office onto Zoom.

The stakes were high, but also low, because I wasn't looking to leave paradise unless the conditions were perfect. I stopped looking at other job postings and figured that something would "speak to me" when the time was right. (I worried I was becoming *Ubudian,* adopting the language and the priorities of the travelers I often mocked.)

The interviews were standard: conversation and a Q and A on the case studies. I don't remember any questions about how I worked or how I created my best work; it focused on skill-based competencies and examples from former professional experiences. The company wasn't interested in how I did things, my working rituals, or my communication style. There weren't questions on how I liked to collaborate, how I gave and received feedback, how I set goals and tracked progress. In a world of "how" and "why," the focus on "what"—what was my approach? what was the meaning of this term?—was alarming.

I left a karaoke party for my offer call, and I accepted the job knowing that it would physically tie me to a major North American city for a period of years. There would be work travel, but I would have a manager, a schedule, and an office located in the downtown core. It felt refreshingly opposite to my experience until then—a fresh challenge for a new chapter of life.

*

I spent my time differently once I knew I was leaving. I fell into the habit of going to the upscale vegan eatery in my neighborhood. It had previously felt like a treat, but knowing I was leaving to take a salaried role soon made me a bit more lax about budget. I pushed the "vacation" button. One morning, I rolled in after going to the swimming pool. It was midmorning, and I'd already swam 500 meters in an empty outdoor lap pool when I sat down to enjoy a smoothie and tofu scramble. It was bliss.

Soon after sitting, a Caucasian man was seated at the table adjacent mine. Both alone, one of us made a perfunctory "Hi, how are you." Keith had just finished volunteering at the BaliSpirit Festival, a large-scale event combining music, yoga, and other health and wellness content annually, and was staying to scope out a retreat offering. We fell into easy, cordial conversation, enough so that we agreed to free a table and sit together. A yoga teacher back in San Diego, Keith's practice included large and private classes, and he was increasingly interested in hosting retreats. The retreat business was a common avenue for wellness professionals to have a high-priced ticket item to sell to their clients. Rather than charging hourly rates for instruction, a retreat included up to a week of curated activities, including food and accommodation. A small markup on each service would allow the organizer to both cover their own costs and also turn a profit, often in excess of what they would earn in a typical week of teaching yoga classes.

"I love teaching yoga. I love being around people, but it doesn't fill the cup in terms of the financial side of it."

Keith was average in some ways—a yoga teacher visiting Bali. In other ways, he was exceptional. Keith had no interest in being a digital nomad or in relocating here. He missed his dogs, his life in San Diego, and his house. He saw working in Bali as a money-making venture. I realized in speaking with Keith that remote work wasn't just a reaction to high costs of living or because of an obsession with the internet. The variety and change and the encounters with other people was expansive. Bali opened doors to new ways of living and new ways of working that made going home feel sweeter. You could come to Bali and take the lessons home with you.

"I think that does break down barriers for people here. The feeling of, yeah, we're all just kind of floating through here," he added.

Keith had just spoken another silent truth of the openness of nomads, travelers, retreaters, whatever you want to call the expats who flocked to these tropical locations seeking something. There was an openness, a removal of barriers, that was both performative and real. It pushed people to think differently and to try different things—to be different.

"I don't even know if it's about costs and income," I said. "I think it's the idea that a good work life is one thing rather than multiple," I offered, inadvertently summarizing what had taken me months to put together. Mobility and travel are one of the ways people use remote work to further their self and professional development, but it doesn't always mean fleeing or leaving home. The happiest people are the ones seeking something rather than running from it.

I had asked permission to record our conversation early on, and in writing this scene, I was surprised to hear my own voice put it to words.

I had found the story in talking to a stranger that I was struggling to tell myself. I was living something I didn't know how to name. And Keith, a stranger in a café, had found a way for me to tell it.

We added each other on Facebook, paid our bills, and never saw each other again.

*

Late one evening, I drove through the Monkey Forest. I now knew to honk before going under the bridge and to slow down approaching one particularly sharp corner. I saw a woman trepidatiously walking alone and slowed down beside here. "Do you want a ride to the end of the path?" I asked. "I can take you to the other side."

"Thank you. It's so scary in here."

"It's okay," I said. "'You just have to keep moving and find your balance."

*

The last few days in paradise felt like preparing to leave for a long trip. I started doing the busy tasks that came so easily to me, easier than stillness, and ran around saying goodbye to old friends. I had my "last" pedicure (cheaper there) and my "last" yoga class (things I might not have time for during work life). It was like I began switching gears back into my North American life before even getting on the plane.

My last goodbye was at the airport, to my driver, Nyoman. He'd driven me when I first visited Bali on my visit to Renee and Steve, a full year before, and picked me up on each arrival. He was one of few constants, and among a very short list of people I could expect to be there if I ever returned. I'd watched Giulia, Alexis, and countless others leave Bali and go back to their lives—or toward new lives in new places. It was my turn to cross the threshold. I—and all the others like me—had come, spent money, earned some online, met each other, had fun, and left. Nyoman's life would keep going; he'd keep driving. My remote work paradise was his reality, and he just tried to earn enough of a living to send his two children to school.

The gravity of my leaving felt a bit like being on the other side of a revolving door. I thought about the future and where I wanted my life to be in one year, or five, and I thought about the friends I had made and said goodbye to over the course of my months in Bali. Some had left and come back, but for the most part, it was a rotating door, an experiment where the results could only be known if you went somewhere else. I knew that remote work, in some capacity, would be part of my professional life throughout my career. But I didn't want to start a company, and I wasn't committed to constantly traveling or being an expat as a lifestyle. As we passed through villages on the way to the airport, I saw Ganesh everywhere—on street signs, statues, in store fronts—the saint of prosperity. My eyes welled with tears at the familiarity of the place I was leaving behind, the home it had provided me to as I tried on a new life and decided on my next steps. I was walking away from a life that felt fully formed.

The world of work hadn't caught up with me yet. There were few jobs I wanted that I could do remotely from a North American time zone let alone out of the office and around the world. If I wanted to work and travel forever, the best way to do that would be as an entrepreneur. But I actually missed getting dressed for work, having more structure, and less flexibility.

As I sat down for the next leg in my twenty-four-hour journey, I didn't know if it was the start of a journey or the end of one. I remember thinking to myself that it would be a while before I'd be back—back to Singapore, back to Bali, back to a life where trips could be open ended and the journey more important than the destination. Moving back to a major North American city meant making investments of time, energy, money, and in relationships that would be hard to step away from for months at a time. It was hard to imagine taking months off to travel. I missed it already, but knew I'd done it. It was time for a new chapter.

By the time the plane took off from Singapore, my mind was already thousands of miles away. The last photo on my phone was a door—a threshold.

CHAPTER 9

ASSIGNED SEATING

I woke up long before my alarm, jet lag stirring me hours before I needed to be at the office. I picked out a simple outfit like it was the first day of school—black jeans and a white short-sleeved blouse. It felt like a new chapter, like a fresh page of a new story. The lobby smelled like fast-food submarine sandwiches. The generic, yeasty smell of fresh bread reliably drifted up the stairs from the basement food court that was shared with a hospital. There were people in scrubs walking toward the subway and street cars, businesspeople in suits, and groups of people gathered around laptops working at the communal tables lining the lobby. On Wednesdays, there was yoga in the lobby and about thirty people went through guided asanas and downward dog, appearing ambivalent to being watched by passersby and gawkers looking down from the open hallways on the second and third floors. The stone walls had a bit more character than an office tower, but in many ways, it could be anywhere. There was a Starbucks in the lobby.

I was asked to be there for 10:30, but out of nervousness I arrived ten minutes early. I took the elevator up to the third floor and was surprised to find the office mostly empty. I rang the doorbell, and a young blond woman greeted me. "You must be Melinda," she said. "Hello, I'm Sarah."

I didn't recognize her from my interviews, but she would be responsible for getting me settled at a desk. *My* desk.

The front foyer had a small reception area with two lounge chairs that opened onto a living room with a six-seater table and a series of stackable seating units that looked a bit like Tetris blocks, angular and amenable to rearrangement. They were arranged in two rows of orange, purple, and blue blocks facing a wall of floor-to-ceiling white boards that could be pulled apart to reveal a large screen. Above, there was a hanging mic, and to the left, a video camera that moved to face whoever was speaking. It was obviously trying to look like a home, but the design adaptations to make it a "work" space were obvious. There was no confusing the space for a real living room, by form or by feeling. I felt very far away from the bamboo at Hubud. To the immediate right of the living room was a small meeting room known as the swing room, because it had a picnic table on sliders. I recognized that room from my video interviews and remember feeling a bit nauseated after a half-hour on a video call with someone sitting on a swing set.

The tour continued through the living room to an open room with twelve white tables topped with external monitors. I was shown to an empty desk. It was long and white, and had some cords coming out the side—hydraulics so I could change it to a standing desk. My desk had two laptops—one of the company's choosing, one of mine—and a large backpack hung on the back of my chair. Among the piles of company swag—a Moleskine-like notebook with the company name embossed on the cover, a branded T-shirt, and a sweatshirt—lay an itinerary for my first day. I was given a couple of minutes alone before I was to meet Sarah back in the swing room for a brief orientation. She was the first colleague I got to meet in person and the only person in the office to greet me.

My schedule was structured: 10:30 meeting with the office coordinator; 11:30 meeting with my manager, and the day continued like this, with thirty-minute meetings followed by thirty-minute windows for me to get onto my corporate email, play with my two new computers, get on Slack, Confluence, and the myriad of other tools that would be important to do my job. The rules for what product to use for what and when were no longer mine to set—I was being guided toward standards that would help me in collaborating with a team. I downloaded an app to generate a security code to log onto a VPN to access my corporate email.

My desk was next to Daria and across from Li. Neither introduced themselves, and I didn't want to disturb them. Why weren't they more welcoming? I wondered if it was common to have new people arrive. There were about a dozen desks in our workroom, and I found it oddly silent. It didn't feel like the space for a conversation. Better to try meeting people in the kitchen.

I awkwardly opened the kitchen fridge and picked out a soda water. There were cheese strings everywhere. Were they for me? There was a bin of greens, some sliced meat, and a few liters of milk. This meant there would be coffee. Where was the coffee pot? The pot turned out to be Keurig and Nespresso machines with pods for the choosing. Despite not enjoying the environmental assault of these small coffee pods, I needed to consume them to calm my nerves enough to introduce myself to every stranger I would meet that day. I was the new kid, doing a new job no one had had before. I felt jet lagged, tired, and a bit like a fraud. I had walked into many spaces full of strangers before, but why did the stakes feel different this time? I later realized it was because I needed these people to succeed (despite not knowing what "success" meant). I was no longer working alone.

A colleague took me for lunch at the pizzeria in the building and encouraged me to order whatever I wanted—the company was paying. We exchanged pleasantries, and she briefed me on some projects I'd be joining. The forty-five minutes went by in a whirl. There was more information than I could reasonably process on the spot. "Is there anything else you want to know?" she asked toward the end.

I wondered if it could really be that simple, if she had really shared everything I needed to get up to speed. Was this what I had come back for? A mediocre pizza, a forty-five-minute briefing, and a quiet, well-located office? I kept waiting for the punchline that never came.

I knew that onboarding, the process of orienting someone to a new job or company, could vary in style and complexity from company to company, but for this one, it seemed to rely on peer-to-peer sharing (over a quick lunch) and the idea that I'd pick it up as I went.

At the end of my first day, I felt totally overloaded and ready to go. I remember thinking that I should leave when I was tired and had done just what was needed to be done that day. There would be plenty of days for staying late, for having a reason to be there. At 4:30, I packed one of my new computers into my corporate swag bag and headed out. No one looked up to say goodbye. As I walked the stairs down to the lobby, I realized that I would depend on my colleagues to learn the ropes and do my job well, but that they didn't yet need me. My role was strictly functional; I was there to do a job, not to share in life experiences and discovery. It felt finite, limiting, and a bit claustrophobic, as if the stakes for this job that I'd left so much for had been mistakenly elevated. Was I just a new cog in a wheel? I felt vulnerable and anonymous and relieved to go home.

The following mornings I'd get into the office around eight. The hall lights would be off, and I'd walk through the living room and into my workspace, flooded with morning light and the din of morning traffic. This was my favorite time at the coworking spaces, too, when I could be alone with my thoughts for a few moments before watching the day unfold before me.

Time moved differently now that it was structured around traditional working hours. The expansive time I'd experienced in Bali felt far away, and I lost track of each passing moment. Days blended into each other, and the workday spilled into the evenings I spent apartment hunting and finding furniture. I thought returning to somewhere I'd previously lived would be easier than starting fresh, but in many ways it was harder. During the years I was gone, people's social circles had changed and tightened—friends married, had kids, and were in different stages of life. I wrongly imagined that I'd be able to easily rejoin social circles, that my return would be a welcome homecoming. Instead, I realized I needed to create new relationships, which would take work. My days were fuller, but in some ways also more empty.

I thought taking a job like this would feel like progress, but it actually felt like a step back. My quality of life changed dramatically, and my focus shifted from what really mattered—my health, my relationships, and my happiness—to work. I was left wondering if those feelings were just the pains of settling in.

*

In rejoining the desked world, where I would go to work was a major consideration. My previous jobs had all brought me into buildings like this, but always as a visitor. These big, bright offices were now part of my everyday routine. In my new workplace, I was just one of the hundreds of people who walked the halls, smelled the freshly baked bread, and sat down at my desk to start the workday. One of the privileges of working remotely was that I was always in control of my physical working environment. I used that flexibility to work from interesting and distinctive places that were usually a short walking distance from my home.

Commutes had long been a necessity of workers who lived outside walking distance of their workplaces. The commutable distance had been ever expanded by transit (subway, buses, and light rail systems) that made it feasible for workers to live in more affordable bedroom communities or exurbs and commute to work in the city. This allowed for everyone, regardless of their income, to be able to work in the expensive downtown core, but it often meant that after hours there was little left. The streets became quiet after six. The buzz that populated them from nine to five diminished the tall office towers to ghost closets by dusk.

As the weeks and months of commuting went by, the more I thought about my preferences in relation to the commute. Would I like to try living in a different neighborhood? How far was it from the subway? Would I consider taking a job at a different company? Seems like a cool place, but shitty commute. These sort of mundane considerations had always been on my periphery, but they weren't foundational to my daily life. I looked at the workers making minimum wage in the cafeteria and wondering how many hours it took them to get there, to serve me a sandwich I'd feel guilty about buying later in the afternoon. The twelve-dollar salad always left me feeling placated but sad, primed for a trip to the company kitchen for some trail mix. My worldview and preferences became shaped by office buildings. Work moved to the central organizing concept of my location and time. How did it happen so quickly?

I had some colleagues who loved commuting and relished the hour-long trip to and from the office as time to read, reflect, and distance themselves from the mindset of work. For others, it was the mundane reality of having a job, the unexpected side effect. One that workers simply coped with—and complained about—especially when the train was delayed or the subway car was too crowded. For me, even my short commute was an endless source of logistics. I wouldn't like it when it rained, but I'd consider walking to take the train if it was snowing, but only if it came on time. The walk to work was the easiest exercise to structure into my day. But it was also the first thing to go if I felt overwhelmed. If I was running a bit late or needed that extra morning prep time, I might even consider taking an Uber. There were many things I invested in for the sake of convenience, which slowly steeped their way into my life and spending habits. There was a pair of heels I kept in my desk, because they were impractical for commuting but sometimes needed for meetings. There were the two loaded subway cards—one in my bag and one in my coat, in case I somehow forgot one. There was the corner café, right in front of the streetcar stop where I'd sometimes get a muffin and a coffee before work if I was particularly hungry or felt like treating myself to a better coffee than the office option. These small rituals became pleasures when they weren't sources of aggravation. When I was fully present, there was some joy in just doing them. But when they interfered with my perceived convenience, they were a headache, just another thing to manage.

When I traveled, I loved public transit, the mundane riding of the bus or the catching of the commuter train was a thrilling experience of people watching, logistics, and cultural values playing out at street level—were people polite and organized? Did they speak to one another even when in a rush? Transit was a living microcosm of any city. Singapore was orderly with efficient tap card systems and timely buses. Their subway, snaking and comprehensive, was beautifully built, well architected, and exceedingly clean. San Francisco was a haphazardly stitched together network of light rail, buses, and subway that belonged to different service providers. The patchwork system had this sort of discoordination that I'm sure convinced many to instead take the commuter buses to and from the city in the South Bay, bypassing public infrastructure entirely. Being a commuter didn't put me off public transit, but it did make me frustrated when there weren't more options. How was transit not a number one priority, given how it shapes our experiences of cites and work life? Was the transit the problem—or the office? We shape the city once, then it shapes us. It felt much like a job: you pick one, then it shapes every other decision in your life.

*

The journey to the modern office started in the homes of small business owners and shopkeepers. For several hundred years, it was common for spaces to be dual purpose, containing both domestic and commercial spaces. They were called work-homes, and they played an important role in the pre-Industrial Revolution economy. Words like "alehouse" and "bakehouse," still popular today, allude to this distant past. Walk through London, or even a newer city like Toronto, and look for buildings, particularly on corners, that have one style of architecture at street level and another on top. The big open windows, verandas, and commanding presence at street level might make you think it used to be store of some sort. The upper levels often blend into the rest of the cityscape and would have once been the dwelling of the shopkeeper. This was a work-home. Workhouses, on the on the other hand, offered accommodation and employment to those who couldn't support themselves financially and were often state-sponsored venues to alleviate poverty (usually in miserable conditions).

This distinction between house and home is significant. Work-homes were created by and tended to the needs of the work of the owners. Workhouses were venues for the economically downtrodden to work for the right to basic needs like food. Working from within one's place of dwelling has always been a privilege afforded to the economic upper class.

By the twentieth century, the building that combined dwelling and workplace became nameless. "Work" was taken out of the equation entirely, and "house" came to mean a building in which we cook, eat, sleep, and enjoy leisure time. There were workplaces and homes, but the idea of blended spaces was removed from the cultural vocabulary.

It was only during the Industrial Revolution and the first advent of automation that workers began readily leaving their home to "go to work." Work was a place, rather than an activity one did from within the home.

Factory work required for employees to be on site and to have fixed hours. Propriety equipment and machinery made jobs very hard to leave for employees, who learned specialized skills that weren't easily transferable. Employers became more rich and more powerful; and workers began to found unions to fight for their collective rights, including fair pay and safety standards. This was also the time period that birthed the idea of commuting, since workers had to get to and from their new workplaces.

Changes in zoning resulted in housing developments being moved farther and farther from urban centers, and therefore many places of work. The seedlings of a middle class emerged and with it a demand for housing. Britain's Garden City movement, rooted in the idea of purpose-built residential developments surrounded by green belts, started a cultural movement toward what we now understand to be suburbs: low-density developments within commutable distance of urban centers. These developments may look like towns themselves, but they often lack the infrastructure and cultural distinctiveness afforded to their nearby urban center.

The movement toward a standard eight-hour workday was nothing short of revolutionary. In 1593, Philip II of Spain established an eight-hour workday by the royal Ordinances of Philip II. It established that workers from factories and fortifications:

> . . . will work eight hours a day, four in the morning, and four in the afternoon in fortifications and factories, which [the hours] are to be made, distributed at the most convenient times to get rid of the rigor of the sun, [and] more or less what seems to [be right to] the engineers, so that not missing a point of the possible [work], it is also attended to ensure their health and conservation.[4]

At the start of the nineteenth century, the famed social reformer and textile manufacturer Robert Owen raised the demand for a ten-hour workday, which he then implemented in his "socialist" enterprise at New Lanark, Scotland. The cotton mill owners developed housing for mill workers near the factory, and New Lanark is now heralded as one of the earliest examples of urban planning. However, by 1817, Owen had revised his demands and coined the slogan "Eight hours labor, Eight hours recreation, Eight hours rest."

In 1847, English women and children were granted a ten-hour workday, and French workers won the twelve-hour workday as a result of the February revolution of 1848. Prior to these reforms, it had been common for workers to toil six days a week, for ten to sixteen hours at a time.

In the context of the early twentieth century, this makes sense—the building technology to support high-density buildings wouldn't have been there yet, and people with newfound purchasing power were naturally attracted to areas where they could have their own home. The ability to afford life in such a suburb and the cultural cache that would have come with it—that of economic and social mobility—would have been powerful status symbols. Yes, in fact, these preferences set the stage for future waves of development. Just as workers began settling outside urban cores during the Industrial Revolution, the want for space away from one's employer continued into WWII and the post-war period.

The next major change to the nature of work came at the conclusion of WWII, which kicked off a major boom period. Marked by a rise in corporate headquarters, larger office spaces, and cramped aisles of beige cubicles, this period marked a significant reordering of the workforce. Workers transitioned from shifts in factories to commuting to office spaces, and shift times became standardized.

As purchasing power rose and the need for the implements of war readjusted the labor distribution in the post-war economy, workers also gained something new: job mobility. New desk workers could bring the tools of their trade to many positions and change jobs more readily. And despite the growth in mobility between jobs, there was no doubt that work was done in an office. The flow of information depended on in-person communication and work allocation. This period of time almost appears satirical in modern TV dramas like *Mad Men* that give image to this long-gone time of secretaries and visible hierarchies (let alone smoking in the workplace). But this was the way of work—it had to take place in the office because that's where the work was. Files, communiqués, and written communication required both human and technical infrastructure—typewriters. The complex web of interdependence that we now manage on Trello boards, email, and Slack was all in person and done in files that one needed to be in the office to access.

There was a line between the workplace and the home, and the place to do work was in your cubicle, at your desk. The desk was a space of professional belonging. The eight-hour work day was born.

*

At 5:30 p.m. on a muggy July afternoon, my colleagues were milling in and out of the office kitchen. There was a crumpled printout taped to the front of the dishwasher reminding employees how to correctly pack their mugs. The dull hum of the fridge was drowned out by the clinking of glasses and muffled goodbyes as people packed up for the day. The office kitchen was the physical watercooler expanded over two six-seater tables, a long butcher block island, and a family-sized fridge.

I set up my laptop on the island counter to trick myself that I was in café rather than working late. Daria asked what I was reading while she boiled water. She steeped a cup of tea and suggested I join the reading group that she'd started. She immigrated from Iran to do her master's and later, her PhD. This was her first job in the industry and her first time working in a non-academic environment.

Min came into the kitchen to make a small salad and joined my conversation with Daria. Min wore coke-bottle glasses and was quiet and smiley. She started working here right after her master's and had become close friends with another colleague, Li, also an immigrant from China. They often hung on each other's arms and loosely grasped at each other's clothes. They had an active physical connection that was not very common in the North American workplace; it felt more intimate than most people would allow. They seemed like they'd known each other forever, but they just met when they started working here six months ago. Fast friends could be found in many places. I reminded myself that I didn't take the job for a social experience; making friends would be a bonus, if it happened to me.

The average age in the office was early thirties, and most people had similar academic histories. Almost all had four-year undergraduate degrees in STEM fields, followed by a master's and PhD in either physics, computer science, or engineering. This was not a community one could join quickly. My arts degree felt like less of a credential than my five years building a startup company. I was there because I knew how to design and sell products to big companies, not because I could build them. I could not code a line.

Because most people were coming from academia, the office had a bit of the sterility of a lab, which is to say it was very, very quiet. Most people spent their time alone running experiments and reporting back to their team or supervisor through routine, scheduled meetings. After my first week of work, desks were rearranged and my team was moved to sit with the operations team—separated from the researchers and engineers. There, it was possible to feel all alone through the course of a workday, totally absorbed in the specificities of one's own work. The action—if you can call it that—happened in meetings: defined times and spaces of rapid activity and real-time collaboration. Despite much of the work being asynchronous, meetings were inflection points in a weekly or monthly workflow. It's where teams realigned their priorities, recapped their progress, and planned their next steps. The work couldn't happen individually without effective collaboration together.

And more and more of that collaboration happened online, even when working in real time. Gone were the days of shuffling papers and people piling into a conference room. Corporate meetings are often now laptop or screened events, with one or more members joining remotely.

Tech companies, for the most part, build invisible pieces of software. They don't have the markings of a woodshop or an artist's studio—there were few tools of the trade on display. There were screens and some servers, and the rest was just decor. We didn't work on robots, but I guess some interior design firm thought covering the walls in robot stickers would be fun or cute. There was also a subtle basketball theme running through the office, which felt oddly divorced from the people who worked here, their interests, and what they worked on. It all felt rather juvenile. If what we worked on was so important and serious, why was it so important that our work environment look childish and playful?

I thought that "corporate" life would feel like 180-degree turn from working remotely. And it was—the ambience of the office kitchen was different than the offices in San Francisco or the coworking spaces in Bali. There were no monkeys on the patio trying to steal snacks, no spontaneous group dinners at the end of the workday. But I did miss people drifting in and out of meeting spaces, of interacting freely, of treating each other as fully formed people rather than workers who represented a specific set of tasks. In the coworking space, people acted like they needed one another. They acted like they chose each other. To be there, in that place, at that time, in that country, in that specific town, in that specific space. They shared a lifestyle. The turnover of coworking spaces made the short-term friendships easier but the longer ones harder. I was sure that if I stayed at the office long enough, if I kept the job for a period of months or years, I, too, would make friends and a sense of community there. But at the start, it seemed to me that my office colleagues only shared the four walls of the office. The rest of our lives were lived independently.

On weekends, I was mentally drained, physically exhausted, and emotionally unsure of how to process whatever corporate politics or stress I'd experienced that week. Single and living alone in a big city, I'd never felt so outside of a community.

CHAPTER 10

LUNCH HOURS

As I settled into office life and adjusted to a new rhythm, my schedule was different than my colleagues'—I started much earlier. After a few weeks of coming in at eight to find the lights still off, I found my groove: thirty minutes of Slack and email at home, another ten reviewing my calendar and scheduling my work for the day, then commute, coffee, and the official "start" of my workday in the office. Some mornings, I would forgo the company Keurig to meet a friend at a café in the office complex. A handful of times, I gave brief tours of the office to curious friends or potential colleagues, and before leaving they would usually ask, "Is it always this quiet?"

By midday, it was still the same; there was never a lunch rush. I was often alone in the kitchen, leaning over the newspaper I'd brought from home, as colleagues refilled coffee or grabbed a soda from the fridge and went back to their desks. Sometimes short greetings would be exchanged, a friendly "How was your weekend?" Often, there was a "Well, I'd better get back to it." The message was clear: lunch was "extra time" in addition to doing the real work. Socialization at this office was not prized in the same way as hustle. I worried it looked like I was slacking off by taking a break.

*

During the years I'd lived in the San Francisco Bay Area, I'd spent many lunch hours observing other companies' cultures in their dining areas. Eating together and creating communal experiences for employees was a crucial part of company culture and retention in a competitive, mobile labor market. The dining halls were more like employee-only restaurants, often having décor and staff like one would expect at a high-end hotel buffet. During the restaurant industry's biannual push to increase occupancy, San Francisco Restaurant Week, I decided to eat out all week—at various company offices.

I sent a few texts, asking friends if they would like to catch up over lunch or dinner. "It would be great to hang out next week. Would it be easiest if I came to your office?" The invitation felt normal outside the context of my experiment, and most companies had a policy that allowed for lunch guests. There was no hiding that an accessible location, pleasant ambience, and food perks were part of what attracted and retained employees, and the cost of a free lunch paled in comparison to the estimated average of over $12,000 spent on office space and amenities per employee per year. Food availability, whether you consumed it or not, had become central to the lifestyle employers offered. It encouraged the entanglement of lifestyle and employment by tying our most primal human ritual, eating, to colleagues and office spaces rather than family, community, and local businesses. I wanted to join the catered throngs of tech workers, just for a week, to see how it felt—to see how *I* felt.

I started a Google doc with a schedule and a list of things to watch for on my visits. Zagat, a food rating service that was acquired by Google for over $150 million (before being sold, again), rated restaurants on three topics: food, décor, and service. I modified this format to better suit my expectations of the companies I would visit. I added "corporate swag" like branded hoodies, T-shirts, and water bottles, and beverages, like fruit-infused water, to my evaluation list. Bonus points would be awarded for beverages served on tap—beer was basic, but kombucha would get extra points.

I wanted to eat, yes, but I also wanted to see if a company's approach to food was flash or substance; was it a meaningful way to understand work culture? I kept rough notes and a spreadsheet of my experience eating at well-established tech companies—many of the ones with icons on my cell phone's home screen.

My first lunch was at a Cloud-managed IT company whose name was as indistinguishable as its office. Unpretentious and low key, the office had the expected snacks and abundance of flavored water but didn't feel like an overdose of corporate pampering. Our first stop was to see my host's desk and visit the coffee station, located in the office space rather than in the separate dining area. This was a smart design hack—we were far enough away from desks to not be disruptive, but near enough to be visible should anyone also want a break. The coffee station was the proverbial watercooler. Team members lingered and asked one another rapid-fire questions about their shared projects while someone graciously offered to help me operate the café-grade espresso machine. Amid the coffee, it was clear that I was experiencing what Professors Christoph Riedl and Anita Williams Woolley called "bursty" communication.[5] Counter to the idea that constant communication was key to team performance, Riedl and Williams Woolley posited that rapid bursts of communication followed by periods of extended deep work were telltale signs of successful teams. This lesson applied to both colocated and remote teams: team effectiveness was served by short periods of rapid feedback *and* uninterrupted work in both styles of working.

When we got to the dining area, there was a small buffet with hearty, but limited, options. There were lots of healthy and vegetarian options, and no trays. Everything was on real plates, and we ate with metal cutlery. I bused my own plate to a cleaning station and scraped off the remainders into a compost bin. It wasn't the corporate largess I expected—the meal and the people were as humble as my host, Alice. As we said goodbye and she turned to walk back to her desk, I realized she was in no rush. It was likely that lunch had been another "burst" of communication, and her afternoon would be solo, independent work.

*

I returned several times to different floors of a major office building on Market Street. In the offices of a payments company, guests were welcome for lunch (but not for dinner). The meal was simple, with enough options to find something you really liked without being overwhelmed. The ambience was generic but bright. The coffee station was set up to look like a coffee shop, in the middle of the workspace, and charged two dollars a cup. The barista only took payments by card, which were processed by the company's own product, a process of "eating your own dogfood" popular in the tech industry.

Just a few floors away, a ride-hailing company's office looked like a cocktail lounge, complete with velveteen sofas and mood lighting. In contrast, the dining space was stark, with florescent lighting and disposable cutlery. Meals were a utility—fuel—and folks quickly filed back to their desks. I remember feeling like a visitor. As a woman, I stuck out like a sore thumb. The staff serving food were more likely to be women or people of color than the employees.

On the same street block, a Microsoft subsidiary that built workplace collaboration tools had a collegiate vibe. As we walked past rows of empty desks to the dining hall, it was clear that there was a mass exodus at lunch time. I sat with Ben, a British employee in his mid-twenties, who commented that free lunch was a salient benefit, and easily constituted a couple thousand dollars a year in tax-free income. He also really liked that everyone ate at the same time; that it was a true lunch hour for everyone to enjoy together.

My host Marianne piped in that it had not always been that way— their cafeteria's lunch hours had been shortened to avoid the disturbance of people roaming through the office over the course of several hours. There also used to be cookie service, a literal snack cart, wheeled around in the midafternoons, but that was cut—too extravagant and unhealthy, according to the staff. People popped by our table to say hi to Ben and

Marianne and I was reminded of living in university residence, where residents shared the type of easy literacy in each other's lives and work you can only get from long-term exposure. Here, conversation moved deftly from pets to work topics. It was easy to see that this facilitated serendipity was, in part, the purpose of lunch. Connective tissue is hard to quantify, but I could see it being built. Information was disseminated, ideas were exchanged, encouragement was given, meetings were scheduled. It was as productive as an email but infinitely friendlier. After that hour I could see what I was missing in an office and wondered if or where these interactions could be replicated online. Was this what office culture was supposed to feel like?

*

Many characteristics associated with Bay Area office culture were started by companies like Google and Apple that built large suburban campuses for their expansive workforces. Their distance from urban and residential communities meant that employees could not get to or leave campus easily. But this was a problem money could solve: chartered buses ferried employees from their neighborhoods directly to the suburban company offices, and food services were brought in-house. Some companies brought in local food vendors to internal food courts that the company then subsidized, while other companies hired and staffed full kitchens. If a meal could be designated an "internal meeting," the food programs were considered a business expense. These conveniences were worth the investment in longer workdays and decreased decision fatigue. And it wasn't just lunch—there were fully stocked fridges so you could eat breakfast there too. Without the need to plan transportation or meals, employees could work longer and be surrounded by colleagues from dawn until dusk, Monday through Friday.

*

Several blocks away at a professional networking site, the office entrance was comparable to an art museum. The food was fresh and healthy, apart from the day's special—butter chicken—that smelled good enough to compel me away from the well-stocked salad bar. The lighting made the food look restaurant-quality, and people were almost uniformly young and attractive. Just like the company promoted the idea of increased connectivity and community building, people seemed to know each other, in that "read your profile once and wanted to connect" sort of way. I wondered if it was all a veneer, and if so, for what?

I began to think that these company lunch hours were also a venue for social performance, an exercise in perception management and likability that might not be natural for some employees. The benefit to the companies, however, was obvious—conversation inevitably turned to work topics.

The neighborhood around an office space was used to provide a collision zone for chance encounters and the spread of ideas, but in a broader context of community and in spaces that were shaped by dynamic interests and needs. Now, the collision zone was enclosed by the office walls. It was as if these companies had decided that it was easier, better, and more time efficient to interact with fellow employees in a space designed and paid for by the company than encouraging employees to mingle in the community at large. This wasn't without its downsides. A 2015 study by the World Bank showed that the intermingling of people and ideas in urban spaces was critical to the growth and sustainability of innovation and entrepreneurship ecosystems.[6] By moving the focal point of community interactions within the office rather than in the community, the benefits of innovation were reaped by the firm and not the community at large.

The downtown headquarters of a popular cloud storage platform looked like a boutique hotel. Just adjacent to the main lobby was a café where staff brought their MacBooks, listened to music, and worked as if they were in a trendy coffee shop. Except everyone was *at work*. This *was* their office—they just weren't seated as their desks. Changing preferences, fluctuating staffing needs, and the increase of working from home had all pushed more office designers to think about how spaces could be dual-purposed, and in that way, they made them more resilient to changing circumstances. Some employers even engaged "flexible leases" that allowed them to dynamically bring on or shed space obligations and avoid long-term financial overhead. The design aesthetic of these spaces served a purpose too. Taking meetings on hallway couches or in the café projected a home-like intimacy distinctly different than sterile "corporate" feeling of boardrooms. It was easy to blend the line between work life and *life* life. The office had replicated and upgraded the home.

Upstairs, the dining hall was like walking into a multivendor eatery during a bustling lunch rush. There was a lineup for everything. I felt like I was on a cruise ship. People said hello to each other from across the room, and shouted greetings as they rushed to join their friends or colleagues at round banquette booths and four-person tables. Were it not for the company branded sweaters and backpacks, it could have easily been mistaken for a restaurant. My host noted that dinner had recently been pushed back to seven o'clock, so he was now leaving before that to spend more evenings with his wife. It was unclear if the dinner delay was intended to extend work hours or to encourage work–life separation. Either way, it worked.

The movement of meals from home to corporate spaces impacted more than employees' schedules and wallets. Local restaurants, often situated near workplaces with an outflow of lunch seekers, were forced to work with delivery companies, their slim margins further eroded by commissions. The most vibrant cities of the world were built around central business district where employees would see each other out at restaurants on their lunch breaks. Now, workers in the downtown core of the world's most prominent tech economy were ordering takeout to their desks or gathering in dining halls like the ones I visited.

I went back to the cloud storage company's office for happy hour on Friday afternoon, and we drank champagne and talked about the latest product launch. It seemed to me that booming tech companies should be creating wealth in the communities in which they worked, but instead I'd spent the week living within a protective barrier built between tech workers and the city. But if it had been my workplace, my office, my colleagues, I could see how this level of social engagement would give me a sense of belonging. Blurring whatever border remained between personal time and work time had made me *want* to stay at the office for longer—and I didn't even work there.

Increasingly elaborate "perks" were how these companies competed for talent. Nap rooms, Ping-Pong tables, happy hours. Interviews mimicked the company lifestyle on offer: cappuccino with the hiring manager in the coffee shop, a tour of the facilities, a conversation with a prospective colleague on a couch, a lunch interview in the dining hall. The version of office life in front of me seemed more like a lifestyle than a way of working or managing staff.

My visits to more than ten downtown offices changed my office expectations and preferences. I found myself scoffing at coffee machines, having developed a taste for free barista service. I was elated by the bacon station at a micro-blogging platform on Market Street, only to worry about the health implications posed by the constant availability of high-fat, delicious foods. Every company had their version of the "freshman fifteen." I thought of the companies further down the Bay, in Palo Alto and Sunnyvale, that had established their own bus networks for employees to commute seamlessly from home to office. The buffer—this bubble— around workers in the name of productivity and company culture seemed to strip the employees and their cities of actual culture, of actual *life* at street level. It felt artificial, and it had to be at least partially unnecessary. I wondered what would be left of the companies' so-called culture without the shining offices and fancy lunches, and if all the perks were an augmentation of the employee experience or just a facade.

What started off as a funny, lighthearted experiment in company culture gained traction as the experiment wore on. It was no longer about company food—it was about all the ways who we work for shaped our lives, time, and lifestyle. It hadn't even a been a week, yet embedded in all the "we" statements I'd heard from my hosts—"we have a pasta bar"; "we eat at noon"—was an alignment of personal behaviors and values with those of the company. The dining halls were full of small nudges toward whatever culture the company wanted. More of employees' lives were being defined, *designed* by their employers. My self-control had been challenged, and my belly was full. But importantly, my mental dialogue had shifted from *I think that's a cool company* to *it looks fun to work there.* I knew an office alone was not enough to make a good work experience, but a "good" office was required to make going to an office worth my while.

Now at my first true office job, on the other side of the continent, I realized I had traded an office culture of blurred boundaries between work and personal time for independent and solitary hustle. I picked up sad salads in the office tower basement and ate alone or hurriedly in the communal kitchen. I didn't want or need my employer to buy me lunch but to buy-in to the fact that being in the same physical place with the same people every workday needed to mean something. I longed for a middle ground. I wasn't getting the main benefit of the office; the chance to build rich and long-term connections with people with similar interests (or enough of, by the standards I had solidified in California). I felt alone, like my work was online and my life outside the office walls. The lack of noise come lunch time spoke volumes.

*

On a warm September Wednesday, I left my desk at 1:40 p.m., with no plan to return until Monday morning. I had an afternoon of meetings, then I was boarding a train for an extended working weekend away. My 2 p.m. meeting was in the financial district, and I did not have time to return before my 5 p.m. train. I packed up my bag and decided that I should take my mouse with me. The mouse helped manage the shoulder pain that increased steadily with hours spent sitting. Bad posture and the relative immobility of desk life had started to give me shoulder pain that worked its way down my arm into my hand, causing numbness in my pinky and ring fingers.

Three days of glasses and mugs littered my desk, and it took two trips to the kitchen to clear them. I packed my charger, laptop, and notebook, and picked up my weekend bag. I walked out without saying goodbye and ordered a Lyft from the hallway. By the time it arrived out front, I was in an active conversation on Slack with a colleague in another city.

Sorry to bother you, my colleague messaged. This was often the case with Slack chats—it was hard to know when a message was the start of a synchronous conversation or something that could be dealt with later.

Now's a good time, I said. We chatted back and forth for the ten-minute ride, ending our conversation as I headed up to my meeting on the seventeenth floor. *Elevator A4*, the screen signaled. When I got out of the elevator, I managed to enter the "secured" office behind someone returning from the bathroom. The lack of reception probably meant there weren't often outside visitors, and my host had left me no phone number to call. I walked along the perimeter of the hallway and eventually found an internal conference room with no windows. I parked my small bag inconspicuously in the corner and sat down for my meeting.

When my hour-long meeting finished fifteen minutes late, I knew I didn't have time to get anywhere peaceful in time for my 3:30 call. There was a row of empty desks, and I asked someone if I could help myself to a seat. No one seemed bothered by this, but there were no signs to indicate this was normal. I took a seat and I dialed into my next call. No water, no coffee, no internet—no problem. Hoteling had not yet entered the corporate parlance—I was one of few employees who regularly moved between office locations. When it finished at 4:30, I grabbed my things again and walked toward the downtown train station. I stopped to pick up sushi on the way and treated myself to a coconut water. I was at the train station by 4:45, in time to join a moving queue toward the platform. The walk to the station, like my walk to work, was the only exercise in my day. I boarded, put my bag down, found my seat, and opened my computer again. Opening my computer or phone was a reflex. Slack had become akin to a Twitter feed of project updates. Checking devices for updates was like a tic that I couldn't stop until 5 p.m. PST (8 p.m. for me), when my most westward colleagues were, supposedly, done their workday. As the train pulled out of the station I was back in my virtual workspace, typing my meeting notes and finishing my workday. Business as usual.

*

Most jobs and labor law recognize forty hours as full-time work, and the idea of a nine-to-five job is built on this idea. However, the constant availability of work on phones and laptops has blurred the line between working and personal time and for many have fostered a feeling and culture of constant availability. Just one more email at 7 p.m.? No problem. Quick exchange on Slack at 10 p.m.? No worries, let me pause the TV. The devices that have facilitated productivity online and in office have also invaded our personal spaces and made "work" a noun and a verb—something we can do whenever and wherever. Some call this digital presenteeism or virtual presenteeism—a construct that values constant availability online (perhaps in addition to in-office presenteeism).

Countries around the world are beginning to legislate the right to disconnect, the idea that an employer cannot expect 24/7 worker accessibility and responsiveness as part of an employment relationship. In 2016, French law recognized that workers can only be expected to respond and be available within a range of working hours—one cannot be fired for refusal to answer emails after hours.[7] Since the law came into force in 2017, many employers have entered into collective agreements inclusive of rules for after-hours communication.[8] Legislators in other regions have followed suit, with Spain adopting a law in 2018 that also recognizes the rights of employees to disconnect from digital devices after work hours to ensure respect for their leisure time, privacy, and holidays.[9] The right to disconnect has picked up steam in Canada, with the province of Ontario picking up similar guidelines for employers with more than 25 employees in 2022.[10] These laws, however, come without enforcement (and often without penalty), meaning they're more like guidelines than anything. They can still be effective, though, if they serve as a catalyst for employers to revisit policies, and for employees to understand and discuss expectations. Explicit norms for off-hours communication (and defining what off-hours means in a global, hybrid, or fully distributed workforce) is a necessary conversation to preserve employee sanity outside of work.

My five-hour train ride was just enough time to check my email, type some meetings notes, and eat my sushi while watching a TV episode on my phone. When I exited the train station, now 500 km further east, my brother picked me up at the station. This wasn't a strictly work trip—we had plans to see a concert the following evening, and I was able to use my company's local office to work from on Thursday and Friday.

Thursday morning, I met a friend for coffee at nine before heading to the local office. I took the city bus that dropped me off a block from the office, a former industrial building inhabited by tech firms whose names lined the facade. Despite being in the city's charming Little Italy, my building was the same sort of bustling hub for tech workers as other "innovation" districts. There was a café in the lobby serving croissants and sandwiches, and people made small talk in the cramped elevator.

There was a doorbell beside the security sensor at the entrance to our suite. Looking in through the frosted glass, the office looked like a subway station. The office coordinator, Suzie, knew I was coming and greeted me at the door with a visitor security badge. She offered to place my bag in the cloakroom, then walked me through a short highway lined with subway tiles into the office's main artery. Much like my office, few people were in before 10 a.m.

This office was much more feminine and adult than its main

headquarters, where I worked. There was a cinema room with cinema chairs, and four big work rooms, two of which sat empty. Unlike my office, this location wasn't at capacity yet. Eventually, new hires would fill the empty desks. The kitchen was big, with external facing windows and banquette seating running behind tables for two. It looked like a trendy café; something you would post to Instagram if you saw a place so empty and clean. The office's central gathering space had low, block-style couches in an open area lined with carpets. The effect was warmth and approachability. The meeting rooms had color themes: one was pink, another was orange. Screens were less prominent, and there were no robot stickers. It felt less juvenile and more like a place where adult women worked.

Previously, I was flown in for a two-hour meeting and had elongated the trip to twelve hours so I could have dinner before flying home. This time felt friendlier because I was no longer a stranger to the people in the halls. When a company commits to a national, multi-office presence, it means spending a lot of time and money moving people around. I was unsure if this attitude was born of necessity or just the human reality that some meetings were easier to have in person. No amount of video chat could replace time in person.

Suzie pointed me to a desk in one of the central workspaces with six other people. I immediately noticed that it was louder, chattier than my office. There was a birthday card being passed around and I was asked to sign. My familiarity with the office space and a number of the people there made it feel like a normal workday even though I was in a new place and out of my normal routine. Michael greeted me warmly. He recently relocated and updated me on his move. I finally met Hassan, a new team member that I "onboarded" via Zoom a month after I joined. I had never met him in person or in a meeting since our first call, but he seemed fond of me as a member of his virtual welcoming committee. I saw Sheima, who I'd only ever seen at headquarters despite this being her typical location. Each interaction had a warmth beyond what could be felt on a screen.

The whole office filed into the kitchen and ate lunch together at noon. It was like they each slipped back into whatever conversation they'd been having the day before. After lunch, I did a bit of email and then went to the big conference room to do an in-person Q and A with the local team. We had often interacted over Zoom, but there had been little opportunity for informal conversation. My manager said to spend no more time than thirty minutes—that I had other priorities. I wondered why. Wasn't the travel specifically for the purpose of spending time in real life? Those other priorities were all asynchronous and online and had nothing to do with this trip. On the other hand, the prioritization was revealing: on-site meetings were for the meeting, not the experience of working near or with other teams.

Our half-hour session ran overtime, and I was late for my next call. Unlike my office, there were plenty of empty spaces to choose from. The first room I tried had bad acoustics, despite having a hardwired phone line. I was able to move to another room and take my call on my cell phone. Private spaces were hard to come by at headquarters, which embraced the open concept, and in most coworking spaces I had previously worked in. The presence of options and the ability to exert preferences—Did I want cinema chairs? Did I not like the way the sound echoed in the room?—felt luxurious. No matter where I was in the world, two things felt essential: the internet and Zoom. With those two things, I could work almost anywhere.

I finished my workday in the open workroom and was among the first to leave around five. I was hot desking, and didn't know where I would be seated the next morning. Tonight, I was on vacation—no Slack, no late night calls, no checking my email. I said goodnight to my colleagues and packed up my things.

The concept of hot desking, where a worker will sit at a different desk based on reservation or availability, originated in the navy, where hot racking or hot bunking saw a sailor finishing a shift crawl into the still-warm bunk of a sailor beginning their shift. In office spaces, the practice of space sharing is sometimes called "hoteling"—the idea that if you make a reservation, there will be a desk for you. This model was deployed in some workspaces in the late 1980s and early 1990s but didn't catch on. That was pre-laptop time, when each desk would have a computer and workers would log into their virtual workspaces. This space-sharing model has been revisited in response to some professions, like management consulting, necessitating workers to be out of the office for longer periods as a matter of routine. Franklin Becker, the director of the International Workplace Studies Program at Cornell University, said "About 70 percent of the time, people in jobs like management consultancy, sales, and customer service are not at their desks. That is a constant statistic across country boundaries."[11] Hot desking accommodates more employees among fewer desks and can be a major saver of overhead costs.

Kelly Dubisar, a design director at Gensler, likens modern hot desking to a homeroom in an elementary school. "You might travel to another room for a certain class but you would always come back to your specific group of people," she said. "But within that group of people, your desk could move around. You might have a variety of vantage points."[12] These vantage points could include private offices, group workspaces, cubicles, and open workspaces. For companies with many locations, "free address" hot desking allows employees to pick which office to work from. Many will choose their "home" office to be that located closest to their home. This has also been called the "octopus" model of office development—a group of local tentacles connected through technology, with a central hub or head office. These purpose-defined spaces allow for the ebb and flow of worker needs more than traditional offices, where an employee may occupy the same cubicle or office, Monday to Friday, nine to five, for years at a time.

On Friday morning, I woke up in my hotel room, and entered the subway station without exiting the building. I joined millions of others on their morning commutes, heading north through the city toward Little Italy. Feeling more confident that I knew where I was, I walked from the subway station to the office. I dropped my stuff at "my" desk and then moved my computer into another room to take a 10 a.m. conference call with London. The highly corporate offices preferred Webex to startup services like Zoom. Their infrastructure made it faster to join calls.

My teleconference call created work: documentation and questions needed to be directed to colleagues located in four additional locations. I logged my notes in the web-based note-taking service and tagged the colleagues I needed to contribute. I received notifications all day as people saw the notes and left comments. Collaboration could have happened asynchronously but played out in real time. Even though some of the items were not urgent, many colleagues dropped what they were doing to collaborate with me. This was often the case: rather than getting back to one another as time allowed, many remote teams wanted to appear responsive and instead dropped in and out of virtual conversations almost instantly. It must have been distracting, but it wasn't up to me to manage their time. I benefited from their drop-everything response times.

I stayed alone in one workroom from 10 a.m. to 1:30 p.m. and missed the opportunity to have lunch with my colleagues. I didn't need water or a break or a social touch point—I just needed somewhere I could focus. I kept going; it didn't matter where I was or who I was with. I did more work more quickly than I would have been able to at my own office belonging to the same company. I had been working remotely for so long, I knew not to get tricked into thinking that instantaneous communication had to mean continuous, synchronous collaboration. I was physically unavailable to be interrupted, since all my collaborators were in other offices, and unwilling to be virtually distracted or dragged into someone else's workflow. I just got the work done. No distractions. There was an irony to traveling five hours to sit alone and get work done.

At the end of the day, I made sure to pack my laptop charger and handed my temp key card back to Suzie, who told me I was always welcome and to let her know when I was coming back. I took a call on the walk to the subway with a colleague whom I usually saw at my main office. That was the ten minutes of my day that would have been different had I been in my normal routine; we would have stopped at each other's desks rather than calling each other's phones. I put down the phone as I entered the station and called it quits for another workweek. Being away from my "normal" routine forced me to internalize that the weekend was mine to spend as I pleased, not bonus time for the list of tasks that hadn't gotten done Monday to Friday. Even a change of office scenery had reminded me: there is work time and there is personal time. Too frequently had I tricked myself that work was an unending obligation, something that could never be contained to working hours. This was the first time that I felt I was leaving work behind when I left the office.

*

Bali had given me my senses back after years of perpetual burnout. What I wanted was something, anything to feel as engrossing and urgent as that experience had. And then that new sense of clarity I brought to the office, left me saying "Huh?" My feelings about my new office-bound life were exacerbated (or maybe muddled) by the ability to watch my nomad friends continue to travel around the world. It was like looking through a window but not being able to cross to the other side. I saw all the things they were doing, photo by photo, and pictured myself there with them. I'd look around my new office and think, *Why am I here?* It wasn't the work, but the actual physical spaces I was occupying left me uninspired. Similarly, I was confused watching the Instagram stories of friends in the city or in other similar cities, whose curated highlight reels made me feel an intense sense of FOMO and heightened my awareness of all the other choices available to me. Yet when I met with those people whose lives looked like constant leisure time and celebrations, I realized that there was a gaping distance between their online projections and their private feelings. Below the photos at fancy brunches and private events was a depth of anxiety and dissatisfaction. Some were miserable.

Hobbies were written into the margins of evenings and weekends time propelled forward by the odd wedding or family event. Reading became something I did to keep up with financial and political news. Pleasure reading faded into the background, like my mind was too saturated by information and routine to leave space for leisure. I felt constantly fatigued. The energy I had left after work was reserved for a small number of friends and my family. But like a candle dimming, I started to flicker, going from moments where I would shine very brightly and feel very at home and at peace with the choices I had made and the life I was building to feeling tired, sullen, and discontent. I started to wonder if the assessments of my peers and superiors meant more than my own. The sort of meta-engagement with my own worth relative to my job was new, having only ever been directly or indirectly self-employed. I had never felt so at the mercy of promotion cycles, compensation reviews, and annual reporting. I had never met a challenge I couldn't face before, but this was the first time where I really questioned if I wanted to. *Is this how I want to succeed? Is this where I can succeed?* These were questions I didn't previously have vocabulary for, and now that I did, it was hard to deny that something wasn't working for me.

Every day had a tipping point, a moment when sitting and doing quiet work would be replaced by meetings and rushed tasks. For me this usually came in the late morning; dedicated work time became more precarious throughout the afternoon. Packing up to leave the office didn't mean the end of the workday; many found they were more productive at home and would leave, eat dinner, and then return to working (from home). Open concept offices left a little space for private thought and consideration.

In the nine months of office work, I don't remember asking myself when it would end. I remember asking when it would change or when something would click and I would begin enjoying myself. I didn't know if that was a commentary on the work, which was challenging and rigorous, or the social environment I found in the city, which was time-consuming and logistics-heavy. By the time I was done with work around six, and home around 6:30 p.m., I often had little energy to do more than feed myself. By the weekends, I planned activities based on convenience or invitations from others rather than my own wanderlust and urge to explore. Was it because I'd lived in this city before and felt a sense of familiarity with its nooks and crannies? Or was it because work had become such a focal point of my new life that I didn't know how to mentally or physically leave enough space for other things? As I grew more invested in the work, I became more attached to my cell phone, treating Slack like a pager system telling me when to pop my head in and out of my virtual workplace.

I made some friends at work with people whose experiences outside the office made me feel a stronger sense of kinship, be that living or studying abroad or simply their tastes in movies. Finding these points of connectivity felt warm and familiar but not like the type of intimacy I'd experienced in the coworking space, where you could go from zero to best friends in sixty seconds. I didn't think the language of corporate family quite applied, the idea that my coworkers and I were some sort of happy family. When I looked around, I saw colleagues, respected and valued coworkers, but I didn't know if I wanted or needed to treat them as friends, let alone family. Family was permanent; this job was a chapter or maybe a pit stop. What about when people left and moved on? These normal parts of work life were made to feel alien by cultures that characterized employees as a family. The paternalistic undertones were unappealing. I didn't want my work "family" to become the focal point of my life, or for it to make decisions on my behalf.

CHAPTER 11

OUT OF SYNC

It was a Friday afternoon at the corporate office, and I was out of meetings at 4:15. I carried my winter coat and bag to the bathroom while deciding what to do next. As I exited the stall and zipped my coat and pondered my options—go back to my own office building, work from home, or call it a day—the two women next to me at the sink were mid-conversation.

"My friend works from home every Friday, and it's changed her life," said one anonymous woman to the other. My interest was piqued. "It's amazing! She puts in laundry after getting the kids off to school and is folding it while on conference calls. At noon, she goes grocery shopping, and she hasn't missed a beat on her workday."

"Imagine how much of her weekend she must get back," the other added.

"Can you imagine a Saturday with all the chores done?"

I was openly eavesdropping, bemused by my own good timing. I was a single thirty-something with no dependents thinking of working from home for the pleasure of streaming Netflix while wrapping up my workweek. The benefits of remote work for working parents were in a whole different league. What was a luxury to me could be a game changer for these women and how they balanced their professional and personal responsibilities.

This was the first conversation I'd seen (or heard) in this workplace about remote work and its impacts on women. I had not interacted with a female colleague that day. I had just come out of a meeting with five men, where a colleague gently teased me for the number of meetings I had to attend, as I moved from conference room to conference room. "Well, don't you live the life." He spent the majority of his day at one desk. It was no wonder he said his meetings with us were the bright spot of his day.

Days spent at the corporate offices became a reprieve for my social needs. Finally, an environment where people moved and spoke freely, where yelling across the room to get someone's attention was the norm.

I liked spending time at the corporate office where I paid for coffee and there weren't snacks available. I liked having to go out to buy my own food and to make decisions about who to eat lunch with. Small expressions of autonomy were how I still felt like "me" rather than spending too much time being like everyone else. I was tired of robot stickers and children's balls on the ceiling masquerading as decor. The "modern" tech office started to feel like an adult day care, and I was ready to graduate. The traditional office, the land of the bland, where people came in, did their jobs, and left for their spouses and families had a wholesome winningness, a newfound appeal. A workplace where the expectation was reasonable boundaries between life and work. Sure, the workplace was changing—but so was I.

*

The tech industry's maxim "the future is here, it's just not evenly distributed" (coined by sci-fi author William Gibson) seemed to be invented for my new job. I was in a forward-thinking tech division of a major corporation that—in the name of recruiting and retaining the best talent—had designed a workplace that was more mobile, more online, and more like us—millennials.[13] We had five offices across the country, and the majority of my workday was spent on teleconferences, when it wasn't on email or Slack.

In the office, I sat next to my closest collaborator and would turn to him throughout the day with questions and comments. In my mind, this was the much-promised secret sauce of offices: the chance to have real-time, face-to-face conversations and to be in an ongoing dialogue— bursty communication. My manager and office manager felt differently and told us we were being disruptive and to take each other into the hall for short conversations. But weren't those conversations the purpose of an office? It was hard to tell what part of this was a feature or a flaw. And I wondered whose needs were being served by enforcing silence.

If the goal was to work in silence, why weren't we working at home or in private spaces that we could control? Why was I in an office with over ten other people? Why weren't there rooms where conversation was expected? And why was the need for collaborative or conversational space the exception in a shared office environment? The biggest thing shaping my employee experience was the office space itself and the ways it made my life and work harder, rather than easier. I wasn't the only person entitled to their ideal work environment.

I felt like I had one foot in each world of work—the new, remote-friendly one and the old, stodgy corporate one. The company policy aligned with the social expectation that work hours were nine to five, and those hours were to be worked from the office environment barring extenuating circumstances like illness or medical appointments. The practice was different. People had different working preferences. Many were night owls, preferring to work far into the wee hours, sleep in, and arrive at the office for noon or one o'clock meetings.

For those of us who had more conventional schedules and preferred to work in the morning, this posed a few challenges. I was seldom able to meet with my colleagues prior to noon. Their availability was simply different. Varying time zones further limited overlap for collaboration. I adapted my workflow around these colleagues' preferences. It meant that the structure of my workday was partially dictated by others' availability.

No one openly acknowledged the volume of work that could (and should) happen asynchronously—so, no one was telling me how to make the most of my remote-ish workday. I didn't book meetings before 10 a.m. to allow for late sleeping and morning coffee dates. I didn't let myself linger over another thirty or sixty minutes at work if a meeting ended after 4:45. I took it as my cue to leave. I saw myself setting defensive boundaries about my time and attention like I worked for a traditional corporation, which I did, while still taking advantage of the privileges my relative flexibility afforded. But I didn't have a sense of identity or personal calling attached to the work. I spent some time looking for it, though. The years in the gig and startup economy had let me too willfully blur the line between hobbies and potential sources of income. The hustle had made me think everything I touched should be compensated, that every asset could be rented for a fee, that every valuable piece of advice I had to offer was able to, and should, be monetized.

The forty-hour workweek, even when it stretched to forty-five or fifty hours, left me other time to do things that weren't for money. But oddly, my instincts drove me back toward a life of blending work and personal time. I spent evenings googling business ideas and early mornings pursuing professional connections into other potential jobs or contracts. I told myself it was to supplement, to find things that were more expressive of my skills and personality than just my nine-to-five job. But the reality was probably that I wanted an insurance policy against rage quitting.

I had grown deeply familiar with other ways of working, be they asynchronous or remote—ways that would allow me to have more autonomy over my time and to exert more preference on the type of working conditions that would let me feel engaged by my work, rather than constrained by it. What were my other options? How soon was too soon to switch jobs? But I'm already here, I thought about the city I'd moved to for this very job. Was there a name for the misery in knowing something was not enough and doing it anyway? Those months, I walked the corporate treadmill, putting one foot in front of the other like a good soldier. It was draining. And my frustration grew as I thought this was just the way things were and needed to be. Was I creating artificial constraints about what was next?

I had morphed into a weary office person, and work had become the organizing factor of my life. I realized I had nothing of note to look forward to. My world became smaller, and I began counting down the days to vacation, like that would be when I could finally feel fulfilled. Like I had to earn the right to enjoy my life.

CHAPTER 12

IN SYNC

While I was becoming an office person, we were also becoming a hybrid company. We had people in and out of the office, in different locations, and company-wide announcements were made virtually to ensure equal access to information. Our meetings had virtual and in-person participants, linked by a video or conference call. That was the definition of hybrid—having even one person in a meeting or group interaction in a different physical location than another group or the majority.

To many, the distinction between a meeting and a hybrid meeting may have been negligible—many teams and companies were accustomed to straddling different environments and utilizing group call services like Webex and Zoom to connect participants in different locations. Within one meeting, there could be a group or groups sitting in a shared physical location, people joining by video conference able to see the convened group, themselves present on a screen, and participants joining by audio only, unable to see the meeting but able to hear and participate verbally. The options meant that a work "meeting" could in fact be three or several different meetings happening simultaneously: the meeting happening between the in-person participants; the shared video conference and interaction with a shared virtual image; and the audio-only conversation that traps only communicated voices, perhaps interacting freely without moderation.

GitLab, a leader in remote work practices, recommends that if hybrid calls must happen, everyone should use their own camera, headset, and screen—even if they're sitting in the same space. The idea here is to ensure that everyone on the call is on the same playing field and having the same call experience, and to take steps to create an all-remote call even if people are gathered in groups. Technology has also evolved to better allow for hybrid meetings, with cameras that move to whoever is speaking to optimize the meeting experience for those joining from home or out of office.

Even in teams with a high amount of group cohesion and respect, the social dynamics of having a visible group of people can create an in-group and an out-group, with participants having to go out of their way to ensure the participation of those calling in from other locations. The "observer effect" is more likely to happen in these situations—"participating" in a meeting to simply watch a conversation, rather than participating in it. This format of passive observation can be effective if specifically utilized, like on the app ClubHouse or listening to a podcast or panel discussion. But if this becomes the standard format of meetings, it can lead to perpetual disengagement and acknowledgment that some, many, or all meetings are useless.

The reality of my experience working in an office was that all calls were hybrid. The transit time between office locations was sometimes insurmountable, and for practical reasons, it made sense to get on the phone or video call. There was always someone who was remote—be it in another office nearby or in another city. True colocation wasn't the practice—it wasn't even possible. This was the reality of working for a large organization: there was never going to be one experience of working for the big company, regardless of efforts. And we never talked about remote or hybrid work; it wasn't part of the vocabulary. Policies and employment standards were the backbone of the employee experience. The reality of the day-to-day experience was held culturally in the actions of teams. The challenges of hybrid meetings were considered the realities of doing business, and the practice was to move across the city or fly across the company for short in-person interactions to overcome the challenges of hybrid work.

In many offices, hybrid calls were a daily reality, as teams were spread across many offices and required participation from teammates or vendors working in different locations. Comfort with virtual formats often split along age and generation demographics, with senior management often having less comfort with virtual formats and prizing in-person participation. This is the same logic that leads many to want to work at a company head office: more time and visibility to professionals in and outside one's own firm. It's amazing how much easier it is to stay on default settings; how much time, work, and process is involved in meaningful change. Why haven't our management tactics evolved to acknowledge this as a specific part of working practices?

*

The geographic concentration of economic activities increases labor mobility and allows professionals to continually seek wage and seniority progression without needing to move locations. A corporate headquarters is a core actor in organizational design and has myriad functions, potentially including taxes, law, communication technology, and human resources. They are also often home to the top-management team or the C-suite of an organization, and engage in strategy implementation, control, vertical, and horizontal information flows, and "tasks dedicated to maintaining coordination and cooperation across the hierarchy."[14] Typically, it is the top-management team that takes action when a new strategic initiatives require changes in organizational design—inclusive of policies that impact how and where people work.

Research on the functioning of top-management teams and organizational theory, which studies hierarchical organization and phenomena like departmentalization, decision rights, and modes of communication, are imperfectly connected and maladapted to specifically consider the advent of a mass transition to remote work within their organizational and management structures.[18] Firms that are most vocal about remote work practices and the specific organizational design practices that are conducive to the success of remote teams are companies that have skin in that game—many of them are companies building tools to facilitate remote work. The impression that remote work is a niche is easier to understand within this worldview: there was no one moving the best practices from all-remote teams into "traditional" office environments that are increasingly characterized by hybrid and remote elements as part of their normal functions. Pre-pandemic, it was estimated that only 4 percent of workers would engage in a virtual or hybrid meeting in the run of a week.

Although there is a dearth of research connecting what we know about the role of corporate headquarters and the functioning of hybrid and all-remote teams, research suggests that many companies across the US have gone through a process of delayering.[16] Delayering, or flattening, is the removal of management hierarchy or the layers between lowest and highest levels in an organization. In fact, research by Danish researcher Nicolai J. Foss and his colleagues suggest that the movement toward flat management structures "does not necessarily mean that decision rights have been delegated downstream in the hierarchy." In other words, delayering does not necessarily mean individual empowerment.[17] Foss' research of over 160 senior managers in Europe suggests a move toward digitalization can actually lead to an expanded role for headquarters and a concentration of power among top managers.[18] With layers of mid-management removed, those at the top enjoy additional power and decision-making authority.[19] Communication can flow directly to the virtual front lines, and executives can more easily exert influence—for better, and for worse.

Endorsements of remote and alternative work arrangements read like rejections of cities and late-stage capitalism. Chris Herd, an American entrepreneur, started his company First Base to help companies go remote. Part sales pitch, part lifestyle advocate, Herd preaches the benefits of remote work and the drawbacks of city-living to his nearly 55,000 Twitter followers (at time of publication).[20] "Remote work in a reaction against: expensive cities, time in office as KPI, bad middle management, wasting our lives commuting, having no time for friends/family, letting our health/well-being suffer, lower quality of life than we deserve," he tweeted.

He predicts that the 2020s will be known as the "remote work" decade. He believes quality of life is fundamentally improved by remote work: shorter commutes, ability to live in lower-cost cities, more time for hobbies and family. These are much aligned with the benefits Jack Nilles saw in telecommuting back in the '70s. The tools to do this have changed, but the lifestyle benefits to the worker have been very consistent over the last four decades. Despite being positioned as the "future" of work, the benefits to the worker have been remarkably consistent.

Remote work also benefits employers through productivity enhancement. Asynchronous work, constant presence (via tools like Slack, video chat, or always-on mics, like in video games), and focus on output are three benefits Herd (and many others) believes employers will experience when they build or invest in remote workforces.

Asynchronous work—the idea that collaboration can happen non-simultaneously in such a way that reduces distractions and allows for longer periods of deep focus—is often pitched as a perk of remote work, but many view as challenging in practice. So much of collaboration and online tooling is built to support in-office, colocated workflows. How can companies benefit from not being able to walk over to Karen in HR's desk when they have an inquiry? This is the problem Herd hopes to solve by creating online collaboration software. A focus on outputs could decrease the reliance on in-office social relationships for advancement and allow for more objective measures of worker productivity.

This might be a bit too good to be true—improved worker productivity while giving workers more time for family and hobbies—if Herd weren't so transparent about the negatives of mass numbers of people moving into remote work. Not just a preacher of the positives, he thinks the rise of remote work will come with specific downsides, like bad tech or a full-on rejection of remote work by more stalwart parts of the economy. Like the buzz for blockchain and crypto that saw land grabs for early profits via a flood of subpar vendors, Herd believes that remote work will experience a surge in popularity so suddenly that technology vendors will emerge with little to no connection to remote work. This could result in the replication of the worst parts of office life. Herd also thinks that "certain demographics and generations will reject the transition. Their benefit—that everyone in the office is like them and it's easier for them to progress—will be their reason." This seems more likely in sectors that may already be slow to adopt technology.

One could reasonably anticipate that a demographic shift of boomers out of the workplace and into retirement will result in more young people rising into the ranks of management, perhaps dispelling any stigma resulting in clinging to traditional places and ways of working.

Preaching to the converted seems to be the preoccupation of remote work advocates. People who love remote work are also often self-selected, in that searching for a remote job or a remote-friendly job was one of their criteria in looking for work. (That could explain why 99 percent of remote workers surveyed by Buffer in 2019 said they wanted to work remotely, at least some of the time, for the rest of their careers.[21]) Despite the self-proclaimed worker satisfaction, the majority of organizations with remote workers do not pay for associated monthly expenses. This means that home internet, an ergonomic desk, a coworking space, or any of the other implements of a remote or home office were not subsidized by employees in the majority of cases, pre-pandemic. Some might argue that a lack of employer subsidization gives workers more choices as to how and where they work and prevents companies from establishing preferences regarding the cost of living in the worker's chosen location. Others would argue that that is a tragic deterioration of the relationship between workers and their employers—that workers are just reduced to their outputs and not given additional considerations or standards by virtue of their relationship with a company (much in the way we expect there to be chairs and desks in an office).

For most of the remote workers I met, there was a sense of gratitude for the opportunity to build their lifestyle outside the shadow of an office building, after work drinks, makeup, business casual dress codes, and the accoutrements of performative office life. Sure, remote work changed the stakes of losing or changing jobs, but not in the expected ways. Remote work actually made employees more demanding. Independence, self-reliance, and flexibility inspired workers to be more demanding and ambitious. That ambition might not be specific to earnings, but it was specific to quality of life.

Whether it was picking up the kids from school each day or spending every winter in Thailand, remote workers were able to build their identities on routines and within communities that might not have been obvious or even accessible had they remained in the traditional or default workforce. For those remaining in urban centers but working remotely, expectations also gradually moved upward, toward more mobility and more options—be that a summer place for part-time work, three-day weekends, or simply the ability to work a few days or even a few hours from home without being guilted by a boss or colleagues.

*

My first time visiting the corporate office, I marveled at the number of men. There were men my age, men in suits—just so many men. I was working in a sector where gender parity receded as seniority rose; a 2018 *Forbes* survey found that the number of women working in the financial sector drops significantly in senior roles, from 46 percent to just 15 percent at the executive level.[22] I was hyper aware that being a young woman would only get more novel as I became an older and more senior woman.

As I was about to exit the secured area through a turnstile, I made eye contact with a man and held it inappropriately long. The man touring me then greeted him by name and introduced us. *Fuck,* I thought, *I guess I shouldn't stare.*

We met again in a business meeting a week or so later, and then another. Each time we'd make small polite small talk, and I'd ask myself if it was flirting. He brought his interns to my office, and toward the end of the tour asked if I could show him the bathroom. I handed him my keycard and gave directions. He managed to get me to come with

him and then asked me for coffee. *Sure, my office or yours?* He clarified
he meant on the weekend.

I'd seen couple after couple meet at the coworking space—people
instantly drawn to each other—and wondered when it would be my turn.
I never dated anyone from a coworking space, but relatively soon after
visiting the large, generic, beige corporate office, I met someone I would.

In the US, 22 percent of married couples met at work.[23] In the 1990s,
one in five couples met at work, although that number has steadily
declined to about one in ten. Despite many spending more hours at
work, fewer couples are forming, a trend that may reflect an increased
hesitance to meet romantic partners in professional contexts (furthered
by the #metoo movement) or the normalization of meeting romantic
partners online. (One in four couples now meet online.[24]) I was very
aware of the stakes of dating someone from work—a misconnection
personally could have ramifications in the workplace. And I knew that
I'd have to tell my superior, lest they found out from someone else. It felt
like an odd and forced personal disclosure. Dating in the workplace felt
like a group project: everyone cared if it went well, but I did all the work
to keep it on track. Once coworkers knew about us, our dating couldn't
be casual. Luckily, unlike the other men I'd dated, he chased me clearly
and deliberately. Our stability and forthrightness made our colleagues
indifferent to our personal relationship, and business carried on as usual.

CHAPTER 13

WORK FROM HOME

Seemingly overnight and without warning, everyone went remote. Well, without warning for most. I had already packed up my desk and loaded everything into a box for a move happening on Wednesday. I left work Tuesday afternoon knowing I'd never return to that office.

While my office was being moved the next morning, I worked from my boyfriend's apartment and had lunch with a friend visiting from San Francisco. Her husband's company had gone fully remote the week before, and she was between consulting projects. Instead of flying with their friends to Hawaii and working from there, they came to visit family. We had lunch, hugged goodbye, and made plans to have dinner the next evening.

When I arrived around 9:30 a.m. on March 12 and eventually found the correct elevator to ascend to the new office, the door was propped open to allow for construction workers to file in and out. The office wasn't finished yet. I'd been finding reasons to work from home or spend time at the head office to not have to deal with the disorganization of an office move that had been six months in the making. Corporate real estate took time to set up—it wasn't a WeWork-style small corporate rental. It was custom built for up to seventy-five staff—or at least it would be, when it was finished.

I walked to the west room and found my desk, facing south with windows to my right. I was seated next to my project collaborators for the first time, and my desk had two monitors I could plug my laptop into. There was a small, locked cubby below my desk. Whatever semblance of privacy this was meant to lend was small—it wasn't big enough to hold a few months' worth of work-related notebooks and the pair of high heels I kept at my desk, should the need arise.

The space looked like a modern office and was bright with lots of daylight. It had places that appeared more comfortable and welcomed conversation, and spaces that were meant for more focused group work. It was as if the consultants asked about how many meetings there were and how many people were in them. It was clearly a workspace, and it looked like it. It felt like the first day of school, with everyone walking around to check out all the new supplies and rooms and built-in video conferencing systems.

At a 2 p.m. staff meeting, we were asked to congregate in the central living room. Despite being a purpose-built space, we still had to wrangle chairs and squeeze onto sofas to all be seated together. The meeting was standard stuff—nothing to distinguish the meeting from any other biweekly staff gathering. Just past the thirty-minute time limit, the meeting chair asked if anyone had any final concerns or parting thoughts. "COVID-19," said a colleague from about three feet to my left. There were two other colleagues seated between us on a couch. The room stayed silent, as if no one had heard what he had offered.

"Preparedness would be good to talk about," I said in agreement. The highest-ranking executive in the room then took over and assured us "the risk remains very low. There is nothing to worry about."

There was a brief back and forth, and I resolved to take essential materials like my laptops and chargers home. It was 2:35 p.m. on Thursday, March 12, 2020. It was the first day at the new office—and also my last. By 11 a.m. on Friday the thirteenth, we were asked to work from home.

*

For those who could work from home, it was business as usual. Well, almost. Stewart Butterfield, the CEO of the ubiquitous messaging platform Slack, admitted to initially underestimating the impact of the virus on business-as-usual in *Harvard Business Review*. The company held an in-person board meeting on Thursday, March 5, which the cofounder and chief technology officer Cal Henderson attended despite having just returned from Asia with sniffles and sneezes. "One board member questioned Cal's presence and suggested that we might not be taking the health crisis as seriously as we should, but his was the lone voice of caution at the time," Butterfield said.[25] By Friday, Slack determined to close each of its seventeen offices in nine countries.

In retrospect, the dates themselves also point to a general lack of both caution or understanding of the global context of both pandemics and international travel. By mid-March, China was through its first wave and

Italy and other European countries were in the thick of a crisis. There had been a window to prepare—how did we miss it?

The pandemic was an unplanned workforce transition that Slack was uniquely equipped to face. Slack had been built as an operating system for remote teams. The massive and rapid transition to remote work was unanticipated by Slack for its own internal operations, as well as the way Slack would be needed by its expanding customer list. The need for rapid communication and file sharing was COVID-proof—something more companies would need more of. Overnight, the company started getting requests to scale up. One company wanted to complete a ramp-up of users that usually took fifteen months over the course of no more than a week. Remote work accelerated across workplaces. Zoom became a verb. The implements of remote work became part of our work from home and remote lives.

The centrality of tools like Slack and Zoom stands in contrast to work that we began calling "essential." Those were the jobs that couldn't be done out of the office—the ones that could only be done at a specific physical place. Essential work was keeping core services up and running while desk workers practiced social distancing at home. Some jobs were essential and some were, well, remote. Most jobs that could be done remotely needed to be. Jobs that could be done from anywhere weren't the ones saving lives.

To live a life so minimally impacted by such a grand upheaval was disorienting. The world became limited to that which I could see on my block. My commute was a thirty-foot walk from my bed to my kitchen table, and save for walks I took for exercise, my world condensed into the five hundred square feet of my one-bedroom apartment. The appeal of my job changed from something I at times resented to something that was a source of stability and routine. Having a job was something to do.

I was the remote work veteran among my peers, meaning I thought the transition would be easy—or at least easier. The context of COVID mattered to my mental health more than I thought it would. It felt like sprinting to keep at a jogger's pace when it came to output. I was able to do everything competently from home, but the exertion felt higher despite the removed barriers of dressing for the office and commuting. While my earlier experiences of remote work felt a lot like freedom to build my days how I pleased, this new version felt a lot more like captivity. I unconsciously had determined that not being in the office meant that I needed to be seen via all available virtual forums. It wasn't even that anything was that time sensitive—it was my own need to be needed and viewed by my peers and manager as responsive. The psychology of this forced transition snapped me out of all my good remote work habits and into all the bad ones that make working remotely unsustainable. The removal of all social life was particularly challenging.

In January 2018, the UK appointed a minister for loneliness, as part of institutionalizing the idea that loneliness has a visible negative impact on human well-being. In the UK, over nine million people often or always feel lonely.[26] There are many ways researchers have tried to quantify loneliness, with one metric being how frequently a person speaks with a friend or family member. It's no wonder, then, that many employers track if people feel they have a friend or someone they can trust at work as a measure of workplace satisfaction. All people have complex social needs that are partially fulfilled by each of their primary environments—home and work. If loneliness is literally bad for your health, social health is the dimension of human well-being that comes from connection and community.

Kasley Killam started her organization Social Health Labs after studying loneliness as part of her graduate studies at Harvard's T.H. Chan School of Public Health. She's been consulting and writing about the subject—the benefit of hugs, the need for community connection, and other antidotes to loneliness—since 2015.

In an article for *Scientific American,* Kasley noted that two different teams of researchers found the pandemic did not exacerbate feelings of loneliness.[27] Actually, these studies reported that perceived social and emotional support actually increased over the period of time surrounding March 2020, when the pandemic pushed large swathes of people to shelter-in-place and limit social contacts for extended periods of time. These results, which tracked individuals both before and during the pandemic issuing the UCLA Loneliness Scale, varied from other papers that used information from a single point in time *after* the pandemic was already underway. Kasley believes that this apples and oranges comparison means we can't really be sure if, on average, people were more or less lonely than before the pandemic period.

"While isolation is the objective state of being alone, loneliness is the subjective experience of disconnection, which means that you can feel lonely while surrounded by people or connected while by yourself. Amid COVID-19, most of us are more isolated, yet that doesn't mean we are lonelier," she said.

When I spoke with Kasley, I asked if this research was consistent with her personal experiences during the pandemic period. A self-described introvert, Kasley finds in-person work environments to be both physically and emotionally draining, but the human relationships they offer fulfilling. "I feel totally content working remotely and being alone most of the time but still engaging with people as much or as little as I want, in ways that I find awesome," Kasley told me over Zoom. Assuming remote work is easier for introverts oversimplifies the complex needs of any person for social connection. "When we're working remotely and when we're isolated physically, it just means that we have to be more intentional about our social health and where we're getting it from," Kasley continued. We have to be mindful, in any remote or in office work environment, to gain the benefits of connection, community and camaraderie. Kasley advocates for intentional habit setting to ensure our social health needs are met.

"When you're working in an actual physical office, you may take for granted the fact that those relationships are going to develop naturally. You have those spontaneous interactions where you're chatting with people by the watercooler, which is the classic example, but even smiling at people when you walk down the hallway adds up to something bigger, which is a sense of community and connection. And in the workplace, that really matters. It's more about finding other ways to develop those relationships."

I thought back to reflections by Renee, one of the cofounders of Hubud in Bali, about how coworking could be a cure for loneliness. She and her cofounders started the coworking space for camaraderie between school pickups. Kasley agreed that coworking is a promising idea to combat loneliness, but not a guarantee. "Being around people doesn't necessarily mean that you're going to feel connected to them. And similarly, being alone doesn't necessarily mean that you're going to feel lonely and disconnected."

According to Kasley, one thing is for sure: lonely employees are less productive. They have higher rates of attrition, they have lower efficiency, and its harmful to their performance. Companies, regardless of whether they're remote or in person, should be trying to avoid that.

According to US census data, only 5 percent of Americans worked out of their homes prior to the COVID-19 pandemic.[28] However, many more were able to—it just wasn't the practice. Work from home policies were often viewed as workplace accommodations or alternative working arrangements, meaning policies to "accommodate" employees with specific circumstantial needs rather than designed for widespread uptake. A 2020 paper by economists Alexandre Mas and Amanda Pallais shone a light on the lagging nature of alternative work arrangements in the US. They found that on average, work with schedule or location flexibility was *less* family-friendly, with women instead seeking to reduce work hours.[29] However, this does not mean that women were less likely to want or to seek work from home arrangements, only that a reduction in hours had, until 2020, been a more likely avenue to achieve family-friendliness than seeking formal permission for regular work from home. This suggests that while work from home can augment a caregiver's experience raising children, it's not a solution in and of itself, underscoring the need for support for families outside of flexible and work from home arrangements. For parents working both within and outside the home, balancing work and family responsibilities can be financially and otherwise draining, requiring more than simply a change to work conditions. Work alone, or work from home, is not a singular solution.

Researchers at the University of Chicago described a "clear positive relationship between our work from home measure and the typical hourly earnings at the occupation level," meaning people who could work from home on average earned more than professions that required work outside the home.[30] They estimated that 37 percent of jobs could be done fully remotely, and jobs that could be done proficiently in a remote or at-home setting accounted for 46 percent of all US wages. Higher-income economies had a comparatively higher share of jobs that could be done remotely, and lower-income settings enjoyed fewer. The other end of the earning spectrum was not so hopeful for remote work. The median worker reported that only 6 percent of their job could be feasibly done from home, meaning the vast majority of workers were still reliant on physical, in-person workplaces.[31]

In the UK, The Office for National Statistics reported that in 2019 less than 30 percent of the workforce had worked from home, for any amount of time. They noted that occupations that required qualifications and experience were more likely to provide work from home opportunities than elementary and manual occupations. Despite their essential nature, jobs that require being outside the home are generally jobs that pay less.

The variation in remote ability also varies among cities: more than 45 percent of jobs in San Francisco, San Jose, and Washington, DC, could be performed at home, whereas that was the case for less than 30 percent of the jobs in Fort Myers, Grand Rapids, and Las Vegas.[32]

The gap in remote work-ability between poor and rich countries is also sizable: the share of jobs that can be done remotely in the urban areas of rich countries approaches 40 percent, while it languishes at 20 percent in the urban areas of poor countries.[33] The more agricultural a country, the fewer of its workers could work from home.

Researchers Bhaskar Chakravorti and Ravi Shankar Chaturvedi looked at the international resilience to surges in internet traffic driven by remote work. Surge, in this case, might be better understood as traffic coming from mobile networks or home internet connections rather than offices with networks designed for mass, simultaneous use. Leading the way with the highest reliable internet for mass usage was Singapore, followed by the Netherlands, UK, US, Norway, Canada, Australia, South Korea, and Estonia. What did these countries have in common? Stable access to the internet and strong digital platforms. Canada had a comparably stronger infrastructure than the US, but the US had more robust digital platforms. Big countries generally have a hard time with this—the vast distances between well-endowed urban clusters can mean that, on average, they have a hard time managing internet bandwidth. This means that urban places were overall better equipped to handle working from home, while rural spaces—that many migrated to—were poorly equipped for online life.

Interestingly, countries that have been havens for digital nomads—like India, Chile, Indonesia, Malaysia, Thailand, and the Philippines—actually don't have the digital platforms for their own citizens to work remotely, and lack the internet infrastructure to support a mass transition to online work.

*

Meanwhile, in my small urban apartment, I was working more than ever. I could switch meetings more quickly. I never had to look for a conference room to take a phone call, and I didn't have to negotiate space with colleagues. In an open workspace, there had always been someone either listening into or annoyed by my phone calls. At home, I was all alone. I could also "book" time with myself to have uninterrupted hours to work without someone speaking near me or walking by with a question. Most crucially, I could start and finish when I wanted. It turned out that 7 a.m.–11 a.m. became my favorite working hours. Ending the day was easier for me than some colleagues, who felt they weren't working from home so much as living in their home offices.

After months of sitting at my dining table, typing on a thirteen-inch laptop with my head tilted way down, I started making adaptations to make working from home full time more comfortable. I bought an ergonomic keyboard and mouse, and a headset that was more reliable on long video conferences. This wasn't enough, though—after about thirty minutes on a dining room chair, my head would inevitably sneak forward, my shoulders would round, and my back would curve. As my workday became more intense or stressful, my shoulders would creep up toward my ears. With no meetings to walk between and my "desk" being basically in my kitchen, the furthest I had to walk was the bathroom. This sedentary, focused workday was exhausting—for me and my body.

In moving workers out of their office and into their homes, companies also effectively down managed some costs to their workers. Some companies purchased the "implements" of home offices for employees and swallowed the cost. Shopify, the Canadian e-commerce, gave each employee $1,000 to equip their home offices. Some, like my company, gave us a fraction of that and taxed it as income. Others expected their workers to foot the bill for having to set up a home office and upgrade their internet. This endeavor became even more costly if they also needed to set their kids up for online schooling (with personal computers and desks for them, too).

As we reached toward two months of remote work with no end in sight, I decided it was time to fly and book a one-way ticket west. I would work from my boyfriend's family home, on a lake and in the mountains. I would be able to be around people and get a taste of the relaxing lifestyle that I missed from Bali. The only catch was that my work was still on Eastern Standard Time. This, it turned out, was more of a blessing than I could have imagined. Working EST from PST was great for me. I started my workday early and I finished early, which meant I could enjoy the sunny outdoors.

And that was what I got—full summer afternoons that felt like days. The workweek wore on me differently because I'd think of Monday as the day I went to the farmers' market, and Tuesday as the day I finished a novel floating on the lake. I had a full range of experiences outside of my workday and was able to balance them all. I played a three-hour game of monopoly on a weeknight without having the schedule it.

There were still parts of work life that felt similar—like the tension over who would cook dinner and then resolution by takeout—but all in all, it felt like being on a sabbatical. Over the course of the summer, my boyfriend was offered a job in a different East Coast city. Would I go with him? The conversations many couples have when deciding to move in together felt loaded by the pandemic timing and the potential impact on my career. What if I had to go back to the office? What if I couldn't get a job in the new city? We decided to move, betting that social life wouldn't return to normal for at least the year he'd committed to. There were considerations outside of our careers—health and safety, family nearby, and the importance of having a sustainable (read: larger) living environment while I was working from home, maybe for a period of years.

As I considered moving to a new city, I also thought about affordability, commutability, and the space I would need to be happy at home in the long term. The list of nonnegotiables changed. Rather than my current theory of prioritizing neighborhood and proximate amenities, I wanted size, walkability, and accessibility. It didn't matter if there was a sushi restaurant on the corner, it mattered if there was one within a walk. I began describing places that sounded like suburbs—and surprised myself. I also thought about the longer term and what my needs as a person, not as a worker, were. Were there parks? What about access to hiking and skiing? The physical environment mattered as much as the city itself when I sat and thought what would actually make working at home work for me. Because even if I switched jobs, it was likely that I'd be working from home at least part of the time.

Actually, that was also something I'd decided. I didn't want an office. I didn't miss those nine months I spent in the corporate office. In many ways, they represented the price I had to pay to signal to the job market that I was employable by someone other than myself. But what it had proved to me was that I didn't need the commute, the cubicle, the coffee room, or the conference tables to be successful. I could be the professional I wanted to be *and* work remotely. There was no corner office to run away from because those were no longer available.

CHAPTER 14

DIGITAL BY DEFAULT

"One of the most common business phenomena is also one of the most perplexing: when successful companies face big changes in their environment, they often fail to respond effectively," wrote Donald Sull in *Harvard Business Review*.[34]

When faced with changed conditions, the problem is not paralysis or an inability to act, but a failure to take appropriate action.[35] Sull, a senior lecturer at MIT Sloan, described "an organization's tendency to follow established patterns of behavior—even in response to dramatic environmental shifts" as a condition he called "active inertia." Companies persist on the same trajectory, as if uninterrupted by the changed business conditions. The article was published in 1999, long before telecommuting and remote work was a top issue for business executives. The rapid transition of nearly all office jobs toward remote work as a necessity of a global health crisis would certainly qualify as changed business conditions. The state of affairs was one of active inertia with companies taking stop-gap measures to endure public health restrictions. It was assumed there would be a date when business as usual could resume and things would return to "normal."

Each time my employer gave an estimate of when we'd be back in office, I realized that we were all in the dark. June became July. The end of 2020 became "probably sometime in 2021." Being able to move without having to leave my position was a timely if impermanent perk.

*

In the first twelve months of the pandemic, few major companies took decisive steps to change their way of working, to acknowledge the lack of clarity regarding when "normal" would recommence. After months of perpetual can-kicking, as return to office dates were delayed and delayed again, some companies made and announced new intentions—they would not return to office and would transition to all-remote or "digital by default" workplaces.

Who is responsible for the cultural and process shifts inherent to moving a company entirely online? Hybrid and remote work requires two answers for every company practice and policy: one for those in office and one for those working remotely. The questions range from the purely logistical to the tactical and strategic, and most fall outside of the boundaries of a typical organizational chart. "When it comes to perks, who will audit every single perk and benefit being offered and ensure that remote workers have equivalent benefits to those who work onsite?" asks Darren Murph. A longtime advocate for remote work, Murph has built a niche for himself as a remote work expert, in particular advocating for how companies can embrace remote work as part of their management practice. Murph is currently Head of Remote at GitLabs, a software company that is digital by default. This job description may have felt unnecessary even a few years ago, but as more and more companies transition to being managed as remote companies (even if they do still have offices), it will become increasingly mainstream. A head of remote, or chief remote officer, or any variation, ensures the needs of remote teams are anticipated, planned for, integrated, and met.

"Remote work isn't merely something one does; it is an intentional series of organizational motions that create a fundamentally unique environment. A supportive remote atmosphere is more flexible, more disciplined, and more inclusive, but it requires a tremendous amount of focus."[36] He adds, "Working remotely is a sea change, requiring a complete re-architecting in how people think about work, where it happens, and when it happens."

It's the intersection of culture, operations, people, talent branding, marketing, and communication. Murph created the Remote Playbook at GitLab and other continuously updated resources that detail how to manage the transition to remote infrastructure. He is one of many remote work leaders advocating for cross-functional leadership specific to managing all-remote and hybrid remote teams.

A head of remote could be tasked with managing the employee experience across remote and in-person teams. The idea is to build a lasting remote future that will create a connected experience between those on-site and those working from home around the world. The key, he says, is to empower people to fill their social quota outside of work, in local neighborhoods and communities, and then bring that culture to work, whether they're working from their couch or in a corner office. "Rather than building game rooms and onsite fitness centers so workers have no reason to disengage with work, leaders should equip teams with tools and documentation that enable them to be maximally efficient at work," Murph says. "We're humans first, and colleagues second."

A head of remote can have varied responsibilities that extend to the in-person realm as well, spearheading in-person events, conferences, and employee retreats that encourage connectedness among staff. These activities contribute to creating a talent brand, or what we could call a reputation for being a great place for remote work.

But what does a strong talent brand even mean in a remote world? And what do employees even care about in a remote-first world?

Charlie Feng, a cofounder of tech unicorn ClearCo, told me about all the ways his company changed their employee engagement tactics when they were forced to transition to remote work. "We were the furthest from remote. If you asked me if I believed in remote, I would've said definitely not in 2019. We got a big office space to grow into and spent a lot of thought into office design and how to get most out of serendipitous collisions between teams (unfortunately right before pandemic)," Charlie shared by email. "However, over the last one and a half years, my mental model has shifted a lot as we've had to adapt."

Their adaptions included how they show gratitude and appreciation to employees (UberEats and other small packages) to how they communicate, and the introduction of "deep work Wednesday." "We tried that in office and it's so difficult. Can you really have a day a week where it's just silent?

Possible on engineering, but when it's a high-collision culture like ours, very tempting for someone to just tap another person on the shoulder and say, 'Hey, can you help me take a look?' and you almost need to pick between the cultures." He described the in-office culture as having relied on high collision and learning through osmosis and spontaneous idea generation. "A lot of this needs to change—we're adapting." All of these changes together redefine the employee experience.

And with no physical place to go, and no colleague to tap on the shoulder, virtual documentation is vital to shaping employees' abilities to do their jobs. This means that information systems and internal wikis are critical to making sure people can navigate to the information they need, rather than relying entirely on person-to-person information networks (and meetings!). Surprisingly, a culture of documentation is one of the least sexy, but maybe unsurprising, important needs of a remote-first organization.

*

After months of being away from the office and another move, I left my position. The hardest part of leaving my job wasn't not going to work, it was that nothing changed. I still got up in the same bed, worked in the same office, sat at the same desk. There was no change in commute, no goodbye to colleagues. Everything stayed the same. What I wanted as the next step was like staring at a blank canvas, not knowing what color to pick up. I found myself in a new city, fully expecting to work remotely, but found myself wanting to do nothing at all. There were none of my go-to diversions. I couldn't travel or even go for coffee. I could only explore them from my screen—and within myself. In many ways it was the self-exploration that many would go to a place like Bali for, but I was doing it by myself, somewhat unguided, and in abnormal social circumstances. The flip side was that starting any new work wouldn't really seem all that new—I'd still be working in the same apartment, with the same home office, same desk, and the same isolation. There was no facade to glamorize, no way to coach myself through by thinking that the new office looked great or the colleagues seemed fun. All the curb appeal was gone, and all that was left was the work itself and the people I'd be doing it with, virtually. I wanted to be like Marie Kondo and find something that sparked joy. But it seemed hard to find.

As the days became darker and we marched toward winter, I made a bet that by the time vaccines were in arms and companies started to navigate back to "normal" that the damage would be done, and more companies would have gone remote—this time on purpose and for good. I set myself a budget and a timeline, and knew that companies that didn't have a remote policy by March were probably not going to have one and would continue to be in the sort of sloppy management mess that resulted in overworked and under-satisfied team members. Any haphazard transition to remote work was going to be this way if they thought merely moving chats to Slack and meetings to Zoom would solve their problem. I didn't want to go back to an office—not post-COVID, not ever—and thought this would be my opportunity.

This in-between was not a heterotopia with its own rules and customs. It was no-man's-land, a type of purgatory. In some ways for me, it was a vacation because there was nothing to perform, but there was no destination and no end in sight. I was able to focus on things that I enjoyed because I wanted to rather than needed to. I realized there was a long list of things I could do, but that those weren't all things I wanted to do. I really did not want to be stuck at home, but I really wasn't looking for a job that would force me to move to be near an office, wherever that was.

For the first weeks, my big change and break from "office" work and pivot toward a distinctly remote-first life included a lot of Netflix. Then came the phone calls and the networking conversations that would normally take place in coffee shops and over lunch. Then came looking for a community—a place, even if just on Slack and Zoom calls—of other people facing the big transitions *from home.* For over a decade, startup accelerator programs had littered the tech world I occupied, "accelerating" companies from day one to day-customers or day-venture capital funding. Now, the latest iteration was accelerators for individuals—pockets of people with common ambitions brought together and "moderated" to share their collective wisdom. This "moderation" amounted to Slack groups, calendar invites, and Zoom webinars, and despite or because of that, it was valuable. It gave me a reason to structure my time, a forum to think out loud with people who were also smart, capable, and figuring it out, and a way to feel less alone in one of the most isolating periods of time: being unemployed during a lockdown.

Worker preferences had shaped corporate impressions of what made a good workplace—or should I say, workspace. People wanted offices to look more inviting, we were told, more like lounges that just happened to be card-access controlled and managed by the company. These spaces, part and parcel of the open office trend, were more collaborative, more casual, more cool.

The funny thing was transitioning out of my job and deciding to only work remotely didn't bring happiness. Even with the tools, the knowledge of the rewards of flexibility, the pro-gig economy, and my pro-portfolio work mindset, I knew I wasn't set up to succeed. Without a community to inspire and support, people to bounce ideas off and energy shared over in-person conversations, I didn't know where to start. Even in a remote-friendly world like Bali, the magic happened in person. The "aha!" moments weren't facing a screen but facing new people, having new experiences and learning together. I knew that it was going to take a concerted effort to find a community of people in a transition, as well as some systems and structures to keep me feeling on track when life felt like it had been derailed. I succumbed to the understanding that in those moments I was average—no better or worse than anyone else trying to muddle their way through the unknown and all the unexpected emotional and psychosocial consequences of living and working in this strange time.

It was only when standing still, when not running from my problems and getting on a plane to an exotic location, that I was able to get a clear view of what I wanted. And to my own surprise, the audit of my choices came back in my favor. I wasn't living beside a pool on a beach, but I was somewhere I loved with someone I trusted. His support and recurring Zoom calls with a few close friends made me realize, for what felt like the first time in adult life, that I wasn't facing challenges alone.

On the surface, my life working from home looked like a world away from my experience in Bali and among other digital nomads. I was firmly planted in a city, had lived in the same apartment for over a year, and did all my own grocery shopping and laundry. But by other standards, it had many of the same advantages. I controlled my time and was in control of my surroundings, however limited.

My pandemic work from home life also got around some of the downsides of my old office life. I lacked a commute and had left my high heels packed in a plastic bin on the top shelf of the hall closet. The business casual clothing I spent years amassing spent time unworn and unmissed (until I tried some of the pieces on, only to realize some didn't fit anymore, and then I missed them terribly). The bad habits of the office—snacking for boredom or distraction were, however, the same at home.

Reconnecting to the rituals and rhythms that had made remote work feel more like living and less like work took time. My time was less regimented given the lack of meetings, but my other projects and writing filled enough time that I felt intellectually engaged, if not "busy" in the way I typically would. This all gave me more time to wander my new city, or at least the walkable radius around my apartment. Whereas I had learned my previous cities by moving through them, going to and from places and exploring, I learned my new city almost entirely on foot, doing quotidian tasks like going to the pharmacy or grocery store—safe forms of masked entertainment. The cheese aisle wasn't just a place to go to grab something to chuck into a cart, it could be a ten-minute exploration followed by wine pairings. The bakery was a chance to expand my vocabulary and waistline. Here, in my new city, this was my "normal." I learned to work and balance my other obligations without external reminders of what "good" or "normal" meant. There was no "old" life to return to. I had to make my own normal in the new city, in the new apartment.

In his book *Range*, David Epstein talks about match quality, the idea that early in one's career, one should try many different things to see what fits both for skills and for culture.[37] Now that I'd had a couple of different experiences of working and ways of working, I realized that I loved the entrepreneurialism of having my own company and the instinct to build and to bring new things into the world. I liked the depth of responsibility and disliked the lack of separation between my life and work. A full blending of the two felt overwhelming, as did a full separation. What would be my perfect match?

There were a couple of constraints on my job search. One was location. A job search confined to my geographical region would bear few (or fewer) results. I didn't want the choice to move forward in my personal life to be a step backward for my career. And the only way to square the two things was to consider remote jobs first and foremost. I, like many companies, decided to go digital by default.

This had the unintentional benefit of serving as great grounds for research as to how companies were navigating. As time wore on, more companies were making deliberate and distinct steps toward becoming all-remote workplaces. Companies that previously had offices around the world, like Shopify, had reformed to be remote first, or all remote, meaning that the default employment relationship would be that of a remote worker. Other companies had announced hybrid approaches where some staff would be in office and others would work remotely. I decided that if a company hadn't shown a real commitment to evolving toward remote first, they weren't going to, and a hybrid approach wouldn't meet my needs. I was unwilling to be on the outside looking into a company with a strong office culture out of fear that it would offer poor support for remote workers and social dynamics I wasn't interested in managing.

It was useful to develop a language around my own preferences to shape my search. I realized that there were table stakes, things that were now nonnegotiable that I hadn't thought of before, such as vacation policy and maternity leave benefits. I became fluent in what I could ask for. And in that way, I was very choosy about what my preferred work arrangements would be, even outside of what the prospective employer did. I began to care deeply about how companies worked and how that would work for me as an employee.

I wanted to talk to companies that would give me a computer and set me up with a home office. I wanted companies that had specific intentions regarding get-togethers in real life. I wanted a prospective manager to be able to speak to team rituals and bonding. Previously, I'd made many positive assumptions based on the physical environments that I'd walked into as a visitor and as a prospective employee, but I hadn't really done my diligence on other elements of the work and management environment. Now, I knew what I was looking for. In practice, what I realized was that the real benefit of remote work was that I could satisfy all of my social needs separate from my employer. Sure, it was interesting or cool to have colleagues who I shared social connectivity with—but having time to make meaningful investments in my local community and hobbies was better. I didn't want an office to become the center of gravity for my life again.

One of the differences that jumped out at me as a job seeker was the vacation policies of remote companies, which tended to be more generous and forthcoming. Many companies listed the vacation minimum as usually fifteen to twenty days, plus statutory holidays of your choosing, plus whatever other days you wanted to take. You didn't have to ask your manager's permission, you just had to give them as much advance notice as possible. The onus was on you to manage your time to accomplish the goals. And if that could be done taking five or six weeks of vacation, that was fine. These was the type of vacation time one might expect in Europe, but it was certainly not the norm in North America.

Employment standards seem among the final frontiers of globalization. Desk jobs have much greater variance in how one is expected to work and what compensation looks like. We're a long way from having a flat global job market, but the increased prevalence of remote-minded companies is providing immediate, tangible upgrades to those who may not have had paid vacation or parental leave within their local job markets.

CHAPTER 15

YOU CAN'T SMELL EACH OTHER ON THE INTERNET

As I considered my own priorities, companies all over the world were considering theirs. Public health restrictions were making a return to office possible, yet the workforce had been changed by over two years of remote work. We were all left to ask: remote, hybrid, or office?

Offices were less changed than the people within them, who had grown accustomed to working independently from home, the cottage, or wherever they found themselves. The workforce was not going back to a pre-pandemic time. Many were reluctant to change jobs during the pandemic, and the pent-up demand for new jobs resulted in a "great resignation" and reshuffling of the labor force. Companies with clear remote work policies and remote-friendly cultures attracted more applicants, and many wondered if it was the expectation of working in-office that shed a negative light on so many jobs.

With fewer companies requiring full-time mandatory attendance, the interactions in offices could be accurately described as spontaneous because there was an element of choice around office attendance. But was the new, post-pandemic office really any different than a coworking space, except with everyone working for the same company? This version of the office sounds more like a community than a company—the office serving to benefit the social health of its occupants, and in turn, company performance. I wondered if my experience of an office job would be the same or different now. If an element of choice were involved, if I could choose when and when not to be there, and when to be home with my dog—would I feel differently?

We're headed in a direction where mandatory in-office time will be viewed as unduly restrictive for employees, and uncompetitive for employers. The adoption of remote work as a management practice and the increasing reliance on asynchronous communication could make going to an office a thing of the past. But the continued relevance of the office, even if simply social, puts pressure on management practices that now must sustain the operating costs of offices and any additional overhead needed to become an effective virtual workplace. There is no longer much doubt that innovation can happen online, as it did during the first years of the COVID-19 pandemic. Workers may not have always been thriving or had sufficient supports, but work didn't stop outside the office walls.

As remote work scales and more teams and companies work primarily online, companies will get more creative about how and where people come together in real life to make connections and collaborate. Their off-sites in exotic locations or on-site in company facilities will play more important roles in employee engagement and retention. There is a new-found role for IRL events in a virtual world.

In-person companies now must compete with the advantages of fully remote teams and will, purposefully or not, adopt more management tactics linked to remote teams. What we long understood to be "office" jobs were in fact hybrid, with key parts of their operations taking place online and out of the office. For employees, hybrid work can be a happy medium, providing in-person relationship building, routine, and work–life separation while also allowing for fully remote employees. In a well-managed hybrid company, some roles or people could continue to work fully remotely. For employees, hybrid work models can also increase the commutable distance and enhance lifestyle options. But why are so many leaders against hybrid work?

The strengths of offices and hybrid work are also their prospective downfall: with more opportunity to build in-person relationships, leaders worry about creating a two-tier system of employees: one for those who are visible in office and one for those who are not. This can leave remote employees—those working from home by virtue, their schedule, or intentionally—to feel like the "squeaky wheel" with different and "harder" needs. On the other hand, there are fairness arguments, where asking some people to be near the office (and in more expensive cities) could be "unfair" in comparison to employees who are able to work from anywhere. Is compensation then linked to your employer and role, or also about where and how (remotely, in office, hybrid) you choose to work for them? Hybrid work can be a Pandora's box of one-off arrangements that can cause disengagement of existing employees or a failure to attract new ones. Hybrid has all the overhead of an office and all the management needs of a remote company. It sounds great, if you're able to do it well. Can you?

Hybrid work isn't an out from remote work: it asks *more* of companies to manage the two different styles of work and ensure equal opportunity for success to employees. If the remote mandate is done well, the office truly becomes optional and a matter of preference rather than a necessity of working.

What we've seen during the pandemic is a reversal of roles (or maybe a reversal of power) where people make decisions in favor of their own personal preferences much faster than organizations change. This means that many people have exited big cities with their pricey real estate markets and chosen to live their lives more in accordance with their priorities outside of their careers. Rather than waiting on employers to create remote work opportunities, these employees have been able to take their jobs with them or to search for jobs that would enable the lifestyle they want. And the more people who have made these decisions, the more companies needed to keep up with them. This has created a tremendously effective shock as increasing numbers began building their lives around the premise of remote work as an option.

Some companies are finally recognizing that they need to embrace the option of remote work. And for those companies, there are people like Marissa Goldberg, whose work lives are defined by remote work. When we connected via Zoom from her home workstation, it was clear she had crossed from beneficiary to evangelist of remote work. In fact, she now runs a successful company, Remote Work Prep, to help companies do remote work better.

She started working remotely in 2015 after leaving what she described as a toxic in-person desk job. She took the first position that was available to her, and it happened to be remote. Remote work gave her control over her work environment. And with no commute for any of her coworkers, she found a greater diversity of colleagues and collaborators with different viewpoints than she often found in an office filled within people all living within the same 20-mile radius. Marissa thinks that she gained an advantage by working remotely that might not have been available to her had she'd been in a more traditional desk job, where clothes and self-presentation often matter more than the output of one's work. This was a recurring theme of my conversation with Marissa and many others about remote work: it's more output focused. You can just *get shit done*. Some people think that core management needs to be in person, but she doesn't buy that. She laughed when she heard of a major company hiring a chief remote officer who actually had to work from the office.

While some long-term remote workers choose not to work from home, Marissa prefers to use different places in her home for different types of work. She has a workstation optimized for video calls with a mic, good headphones, and a webcam. She has a different workspace for writing, one that's away from technology and "much more comfortable." Separate spaces, even within one's own home, can provide the psychological cues that allow for deep work, much in the same way an office outside the home cues you to get into work mode. The element of choice matters: you can choose to work from home, a coffee shop, a library, or an office.

You don't have the same space constraint that you might have at a desk or at a cubicle. You can choose when and where to work.

But Marissa is sure to warn that you can't do office work at home. Real remote work requires a commitment to the working practices of remote teams, not the movement of office work to one's home or the replication of an in-office schedule on Zoom. She advises companies against simply copying in-office tactics for a remote workspace. She says doing this leaves people unhappy and not knowing why. The office has its positives, she said, but some of the office positives won't work at home. You have to learn to take advantage of the remote work positives—your fixed desk doesn't need to be your location, and you don't have to work nine-to-five hours. For some people, a better work arrangement might be two hours on, two hours off. You can embrace different styles of working. There's no one right way to do it, and that's okay. In fact, that's the point.

"Some people will say, Joe's always at his desk. Do we really want that?" She described that trust issues with personnel should not fall on the employee to solve and disagrees with efforts to surveil employees (by monitoring their keystrokes or even having their video cameras on throughout the workday). With proper management structures and record keeping, most people can find ways to be productive on their own time, without the default structures of physical presence that many assume come with working in an office context.

For companies that struggle moving to asynchronous work, Marissa suggested starting from scratch: cancel all meetings and see what happens. She places a high value on deep work time and thinks it results in higher-quality thinking over the long term. Most team members don't need daily updates when working this way. She also says that in her experience, people stop watching or reading daily updates and that middle management at the office are just there for oversight. This fear drives virtual meetings, which is something to work on. With effective reporting structures and clarity of goals, remote work takes out the need for middle management.

Discomfort with virtual management can lead to death by meeting rather than reliance of the written documentation people now have more time and energy to create. A strong culture of documentation (not just updates) is crucial to high-performing remote teams. And good templates and clear scoping should leave more teams able to work with fewer meetings for real-time consensus building. The documents should do more heavy lifting.

Many remote teams will talk about the importance of "bonding," or creating social ties and trust. It can also mean cohesion and alignment or division of the company. Job (yes, that's his real name) from remote. com, a company that facilitates payments and HR for remote workers, had the most cogent explanation of why he likes bonding—it reduces the barrier to reaching out to someone. Once a company gets to a certain size, there's no reason to think that everyone would know one another. It's the same case for online, but there are great tools to help people gain visibility to other parts of an organization. There are many tools used to promote bonding and social connections in the virtual workplace, ranging from Slack plugins like Donut to virtual escape rooms.

But what about psychological safety over Zoom? Much like in an office environment, leaders set the conditions for psychological safety when they admit their own mistakes by expressly asking others to contribute their opinions. This type of fallibility goes even further online, where people often need more assurance about the validity of their contributions and their feelings, particularly misgivings and negative sentiments. Leadership that's able to embody this sort of humility can lay the building blocks for psychological safety.

Moving from the "why" of remote work to the "how" is the biggest obstacle to success. For many, remote work will not be a destination or a full-time pursuit. It will be something workers and members of their teams go to for days, weeks, months, or maybe even years at a time, but not for their whole careers. Just like working in an office environment, working in a remote team or a hybrid remote team is a distinct and separate way of working. The solutions for the how to do it successfully will change over time, but managing remote teams is a new practice. As one CEO said to me, "There's not an established good way to run a remote organization, there's just a bunch of people that tried a bunch of things and some of them work." Over the course of one's careers, there may be many roles that require a degree of literacy in remote work. By focusing on the why, one can better understand the how.

The major transition to remote work during the pandemic was not true remote work, in that it was short-term working from home without the freedom that truly comes with remote work. Some embraced the opportunity of remote work to work from a cottage, turning road trips into working vacations, and contemplating major moves. Others struggled with changing times and procedures in a shifting reality and recognized that for them, the office offered a sense of stability and separation from their home life that they enjoyed and missed. But this was working from home, not remote work.

Working from home is a descriptive of where someone works: remote work is how someone works *without* implying where. Choosing where to work is actually the easy part. The how of remote work is much more complex—good remote work depends on teams, management structures and personal practices to make a virtual work environment as enjoyable and productive as a traditional workspace. If we're optimizing for hours spent working, remote work is potentially a solution: most people report working more hours with fewer interruptions when working outside a traditional office space. And by removing the commute, the worker gets more personal time back, which may result in more productive work time. If employee health equals company health, wouldn't more employers want to explore what ways remote work could be beneficial?

The internet allows me to work from anywhere for anyone, be that as a job or a side hustle. But the idea is that they will not dictate how I make decisions in my personal life. That is a freedom that not many have had the option to pursue, particularly within the confines of a stable income. Now that I have both, there's no going back.

We often forget how quickly some things can normalize. In the '90s, there were smoking sections in every restaurant, and computers were confined to computer labs. Blackberrys were the rage in the early 2000s, and laptops became affordable and necessary a decade later. There are many ways that technology has entered our lives in ways that are inextricable now that were unthinkable ten or twenty years ago. Maybe the expectation of being in an office five days a week will be like that. Perhaps the pandemic was just the tipping point where remote work went from the margins to front and center in our conception of what it means to "go" to work. And the very concept of living somewhere far-flung is also normalizing remote workers, through digital nomad visas being offered in countries like Indonesia and Malta. No longer just long-term travelers, digital nomads are now a category of worker. Similarly, some regional governments offer tax rebates and financial incentives to relocate to some Canadian provinces and American states. These internal migration flows are also being changed by remote work, one individual and family at a time.

I asked Job from remote.com what the core difference was with remote work. "Well," he said, "They can't smell you on the internet."

CONCLUSION

One of the biggest things that's changed for me over the last four years is the sense of stakes of working remotely. For many of the people I met at Hubud, the coworking space in Bali, there was an existential calling to change their way of life that required quitting jobs and restructuring their incomes, entirely changing their careers to be able to live their dream of traveling, fueled by work online. That sort of dramatic readjustment now feels so much more within the realm of the possible and accessible to average, everyday people who may not even consider themselves risk-takers. Now, almost anyone could work entirely online and move locations and be able to experience that same flexibility and sense of wonder that led people across the world to Bali when I started writing about the potential of remote work.

Our new familiarity with remote work, using Zoom and Teams meetings for regular online interaction, may have dulled our senses to the exciting potential that it holds. We've normalized remote work to the extent that maybe we have forgotten the opportunity that it affords if we apply it to our own lives.

In the tug of war between work and life, it seemed like work was winning, for me, anyway. I had followed my professional aspirations in and out of different environments and tried new things over the years. The times when I was happiest and when I felt truly alive was when my life was the center of my work. And for me, that meant remote work.

I don't think we often talk about how the person we are at work impacts the person we are outside of it. Being tired and stressed from work spills over into our personal lives. It's hard to switch off the emotional and psychological toll of the workplace once we "clock" out. I think that was also something people were seeking in Bali. The voracious pursuit of yoga and wellness was only partially to do with yoga and wellness. It was also about bringing that same sense of calm into working life, about being able to work asynchronously at a self-moderated pace, about choosing what hours to work and what sort of tasks to do. By feeling more in control over work life, there was more freedom for creative and solitary deep work. The cues that you can build into remote work through personal practices and structures can be just as powerful as those built into the rhythms of offices and commutes.

The founders of Hubud accomplished their goal of changing how people lived, worked, and learned. The world that they saw coming into existence was encouraged by their efforts and by all the other community members who were invested in the global coworking movement. Autonomy, choice, freedom of movement, and an ability to explore the world and find new ways to contribute to it—these are things that remote work can encourage, whether you're a digital nomad, working from home, or even in the most traditional office environment.

One of the casualties of pandemic restrictions was coworking spaces, particularly for digital nomads who found themselves more location restricted. Unfortunately, with higher rents and fewer travelers, many coworking spaces had to close. The specifics of the world I wrote about in the first section of this book no longer exist. There are still places like Hubud in Bali and beyond that are welcoming back travels and workers of all types. Life is returning, and new but familiar rhythms are falling back into place. Digital nomads and travelers alike are starting to once again explore new towns and new countries, all while working remotely from their trusted laptop. That world is coming back, and I hope to rejoin it, if only for short periods of time.

Jenny, who I met in Bali, continues to travel. She now focuses on what she calls "higher-ticket offers" and getting her coaching clients to $10,000 monthly revenues. Alexis, who traveled to avoid the high cost of living in Toronto, has also resettled now, renting an apartment and working online for an American company. Many of my colleagues from my office job have moved on, as has my relationship with the man I met there.

When I next go to San Francisco, it won't be to sit in corporate cafeterias or visit people at their offices. It will be for weddings. It will be for joyous occasions of old friends coming together to celebrate, not to imagine what my life would look like if I made choices that looked more like theirs. I imagine many of those office towers will still be there, as will many people who'll choose to continue working there. Maybe someday I'll be one of them again. But for now, the rhythm of my life is very much the rhythm of life and not the rhythm of my work. My work will come with me.

For me, it's been four years and probably 40,000 air miles from when I started examining remote work. Is there anything left to say? The last two years in particular were a paradigm shift for me and everyone else, but the impact of work on our lives remains. We've been reminded about the importance of community, the drawbacks of isolation, and the need to focus on what our true priorities are. I can see why after years of working from home under duress, some would say that being in the office was their preferred way of working. But for me, the people who I wanted to see most were not necessarily the ones I worked with. They were the family and friends I was separated from.

As the world opened up again, and I made plans to travel, it was to see those people in their places, not my work colleagues, that excited me the most. Yet when the opportunity arose to book a flight to go on my first work trip, I also jumped at the chance. What would it feel like to walk into an office, I wondered, after years of working only online? And this is what I realized was missing from the dialogue about remote work—how does it actually feel doing it. That feeling can be found online. The relationships can be just as real; the work can be just as important.

I started writing this book determined to not make it my story—God forbid it be called a memoir. But it was clearly me in the coworking space and me observing the ways work was shaping and reshaping lives, including my own, when I took an office job. It was me marveling at how years of remote work had not prepared me to go remote unexpectedly in a management structure that was not finely calibrated to be a remote team. So the story became more about me than I ever intended. Having worked through the pandemic years, we've all experienced one of the most large-scale and accelerated transformations in the workplace since the Industrial Revolution.

The lasting effects for how this transformative shift has impacted our work and our lives will be written elsewhere. I hope I've piqued your interest about the many options available for working in the twenty-first century in a post-pandemic world and provided you with some answers that you may have had about remote work. And I hope, if nothing else, you realize that you can make a choice about where to live and how to work. I'm excited by more people having the choice, the options, the tools, and the flexibility to discover life out of the office, and maybe even around the world. Remote work can actually be about putting more life in your work, not more work in your life.

AFTERWORD

One year into my fully remote job and two and a half years after leaving the office for the pandemic, I got on an overnight flight to travel to my company's office. As I walked in the doors before nine on a Tuesday morning I was greeted by friendly faces I'd only ever seen in rectangular blocks on Zoom. That week we sat side by side, had bursty communication about work projects, and got to know each other as people over lunches, coffee breaks, and dinners. Throughout, we commented on how normal it felt, and how nice it was to look each other in the eye.

Some of my fears came true. There was a velocity of information that moved through the physical office space that filled in gaps of what I had learned through remote work. But rather than disenchanting me with the remote workplace, it made me realize how worth doing that work was, and the importance of the ongoing investment in building a strong remote culture. And crucially, how these small intervals of coming together in person made the work feel worth doing.

WORKS CITED

1. Nilles, Jack. *The Telecommunications-Transportation Tradeoff*, BookSurge Publishing. 1974.

2. http://www.theworkhome.com/what-is-a-workhome/

3. http://www.theworkhome.com/what-is-a-workhome/

4. http://www.theworkhome.com/what-is-a-workhome/

5. https://hbr.org/2020/10/successful-remote-teams-communicate-in-bursts

6. https://openknowledge.worldbank.org/handle/10986/23029

7. https://blogs.loc.gov/law/2020/08/telework-and-the-french-right-to-disconnect/

8. https://www.shrm.org/resourcesandtools/legal-and-compliance/employment-law/pages/global-france-spain-right-to-disconnect.aspx

9. https://www.shrm.org/resourcesandtools/legal-and-compliance/employment-law/pages/global-france-spain-right-to-disconnect.aspx

10. https://www.ontario.ca/document/your-guide-employment-standards-act-0/written-policy-disconnecting-from-work

11. https://www.techtarget.com/searchvirtualdesktop/definition/hot-desking/

12. https://nobhillgazette.com/the-future-of-the-office/

13. http://wp.lancs.ac.uk/everydayfutures/files/2016/08/chatterton_newmarch.pdf

14. http://www.theworkhome.com/what-is-a-workhome/

15. https://jorgdesign.springeropen.com/articles/10.1186/s41469-019-0048-7

16. https://jorgdesign.springeropen.com/articles/10.1186/s41469-019-0048-7

17. https://jorgdesign.springeropen.com/articles/10.1186/s41469-019-0048-7

18. https://www.sciencedirect.com/science/article/abs/pii/
S000768132030149X?via%3Dihub

19. https://www.sciencedirect.com/science/article/abs/pii/
S000768132030149X?via%3Dihub

20. https://twitter.com/chris_herd, September 15, 2022.

21. https://buffer.com/state-of-remote-work/2019

22. https://www.forbes.com/sites/forbesmarketplace/2018/06/05/5-things-you-
need-to-know-about-women-in-finance/

23. https://www.bamboohr.com/
blog/8-workplace-romance-facts-need-know-right-now

24. https://www.smithsonianmag.com/arts-culture/
new-insights-how-american-couples-meet-180973335/

25. https://hbr.org/2020/07/
the-ceo-of-slack-on-adapting-in-response-to-a-global-crisis

26. https://www.globaldatinginsights.com/
news/9-million-british-people-often-always-feel-lonely/

27. https://www.scientificamerican.com/article/
in-the-midst-of-the-pandemic-loneliness-has-leveled-out/

28. https://review.chicagobooth.edu/economics/2020/article/
only-37-percent-us-jobs-can-be-done-home

29. https://www.nber.org/papers/w26605

30. https://www.nber.org/papers/w26605

31. https://bfi.uchicago.edu/wp-content/uploads/BFI_White-Paper_Dingel_
Neiman_3.2020.pdf

32. https://bfi.uchicago.edu/wp-content/uploads/BFI_White-Paper_Dingel_
    Neiman_3.2020.pdf

33. https://ideas.repec.org/p/mtl/montec/07-2020.html

34. https://hbr.org/1999/07/why-good-companies-go-bad

35. https://hbr.org/1999/07/why-good-companies-go-bad

36. https://theorg.com/insights/the-hottest-new-title-in-tech-head-of-remote-work

37. Epstein, David. *Range*, Riverhead Books. 2021.

ACKNOWLEDGMENTS

I'd like to thank the communities that supported me in the research, writing, and editing of this work. Thanks to the fine folks at King's College in Halifax who encouraged me to put more of myself on the page, and whose instruction, care, and encouragement shaped my writing. Particularly Ayelet Tsabari. Charlotte Gill, Wanda Taylor, Kim Pittaway, Dean Job, Megan Cole, and Jenn Thornhill Verma—thank you. Thanks to Banff Centre and the Getting the Maybe program for planting the seeds that led me to Bali. Renee, Steve, and the community of Hubudians and Ubudians who let me into their world and make it mine. Sabrina, Kelly, and the team at YGTMedia for pushing me to the finish line. Everyone who took time to speak to me about their work—the why and the how. Thank you.

YGTMedia Co. is a blended boutique publishing house for mission-driven humans. We help seasoned and emerging authors "birth their brain babies" through a supportive and collaborative approach. Specializing in narrative nonfiction and adult and children's empowerment books, we believe that words can change the world, and we intend to do so one book at a time.

 ygtmedia.co/publishing

 @ygtmedia.company

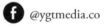 @ygtmedia.co

Made in the USA
Las Vegas, NV
19 January 2023

65888528R00108